STORIES *of* ORIGIN

The Invisible Lives of Migrants in the Gulf

WRITTEN BY VANI SARASWATHI

Edited by Rima Kalush

EDITOR'S NOTE

When Bahraini activist Esra'a Al Shafei launched Migrant-Rights.org (MR) over 12 years ago, local narratives on migration were largely driven by negative media coverage or otherwise absent from public conscious. There was no World Cup in Qatar and the construction boom in Dubai was only just starting to reveal its problematic underpinnings, so there was little international attention paid to the topic. Migrant-Rights.org started as a bilingual blog to document abuses against workers, to monitor media reporting, and to ignite discussion.

These objectives remain the core component of MR's work, which has now grown to include multimedia campaigns, research and policy analysis, direct advocacy with stakeholders, and the kind of original reporting featured in this book. The network which makes our work possible has grown to include contributors from the GCC and countries of origin, journalists and researchers, eager students, community activists, and civil society organisations.

MR focuses on the Gulf Cooperation Council countries (GCC) and its migration corridors in Asia and Africa, and our target audience is those who live and work in the region. As the last few years have shown the world, negative attitudes and practises towards migration is by no means exclusive to the GCC. Indeed, one could argue that the Gulf's migration policies are more open than those of many other countries; that successful immigrant stories have been been made in Dubai, Riyadh, and the other star attractions of the GCC.

Of course, there is an underlying rationale to these relatively welcoming migration policies: the Gulf states need migrant labour not only to prosper, but to exist at all. (And despite efforts to reduce the migrant workforce, a low population growth rate indicate that labour migration will continue to be a necessary reality for these countries in the years to come.) While labour migration policies are open in the sense that there are few hurdles to obtaining a work visa, on the flipside, protections for many low-income workers are weak and access to justice is out of reach for the majority.

Though significant degrees of difference exist in labour migration policies, general trends in the region over the last decade have included reforms that ease workers' ability to change employers and the GCC states have been among the first in the world to pass laws and regulations on domestic workers. While reforms – with a variable scale of implementation – have been made, anti-migrant policies and voices are growing louder, particularly in Saudi and Kuwait.

This is the complex picture of migration in the GCC that eschews either victimisation or demonisation, and this is what Migrant-Rights.org explores and makes accessible to audiences in the region and around the world. A critical component of this picture is, of course, the voices of migrants themselves. The Stories of Origin series endeavours to amplify these experiences, and contribute to a greater understanding of migration to the Gulf.

—Rima Kalush

AUTHOR'S NOTE:

BRINGING ABOUT ATTITUDINAL AND BEHAVIOURAL CHANGE TOWARDS migrant workers in the Gulf States is one of the toughest tasks Migrant-Rights.org (MR) faces in the work we do.

The discriminatory provisions of the Kafala system, identity politics, a never-ending dependence on foreign labour, dwindling livelihoods in countries of origin, and the commodification of humans on both ends of the labour migration chain all fortify a seemingly insurmountable wall of resistance to any meaningful change.

MR's work is focussed on researching on-the-ground realities and assessing legislative changes, advocacy with stakeholders, creating educational tools, reporting on abuses and violations, and holding government accountable. During the course of this work, the echoing commonality is that lower-income migrant workers are just numbers on paper, and are deliberately rendered faceless and invisible both in their home countries and the countries they work in.

How then do we personalise their aspirational migration journey? How do we put in context that their dreams and intent are no different from those who migrate from a more privileged socio-economic environment? How to tell the story without whitewashing the peculiar problems that certain groups face?

The idea for Stories of Origin was a result of those questions: To report from the homes of migrant workers, from their families and communities, from the environment that forced or inspired them to move.

The first of the reports was from Nepal in 2015; three years, seven countries, eight reporting tours later, we wrap up the series.

The biggest bit of learning has been that the motivations and aspirations for migration are identical across border and continents – love for their families and a yearning for a better future for their children. Many have seen people before them turn their lives around after a stint in the 'Gulf'. That narrative is slowly changing for the worse. The success stories are outnumbered by the stories of struggle, yet the hunger to leave persists.

This compilation is dedicated to all those who take that often scary step into the unknown, fuelled by love and dreams for their own.

–Vani Saraswathi

[...]
Where knowledge is free
Where the world has not been broken up into fragments
By narrow domestic walls
Where words come out from the depth of truth
[...] – Rabindranath Tagore

CONTENTS

____

NEPAL

Better Lives, Betting on Migration 14
Returnees' Dreams, Some Interrupted 19
Recruitment or Human Trafficking? 26

____

INDONESIA

Commodification of Women in Rural Indonesia 35
Recruited Under Duress, Untrained and Unprepared for Migration 40

____

INDIA

Indian Fishermen: Between the Devil and the Deep Sea 49
Life After Arrests 54
High Skills, Low Value: Indifferent Governments on Both Ends of Migration 59
Migration in the Times of Distrust 66
Of Bogeymen and Willing Prey 73
Building Trust: Two Steps Forwad, One Step Back 80

____

SRI LANKA

In Sri Lanka, Men are Free, Women Have a Price Tag 87
Dreams...Perpetually in Progress 92

UGANDA

In Uganda, Everyone Wants to …What? …Go Abroad **101**
In the Land of Friends and Uncles, Everyone is an Agent **108**

ETHIOPIA

The Ban is a Blessing…for the Traffickers in Ethiopia **117**
"I Want to Escape" **124**
Battling 'Evil' Stereotypes, Pregnancies, and Abuse in the Gulf **129**
Failed Migrations and the Community Approach **136**

PHILIPPINES

Out of the Philippines: it Takes a Village, and Then Some **145**
To Leave, To Stay, To Adjust…Come What May **150**
Run Sister, Run! **157**
Marketing the 'World Class Filipino Worker' **164**

*"I had said I will never go abroad.
But the situation is such now, I have no choice."*

NEPAL

Published April-May 2015

POPULATION	28,900,00
NUMBER OF MIGRANTS IN THE GCC	883,523
MAIN RECEIVING COUNTRY GLOBAL	Saudi Arabia
MAIN RECEIVING COUNTRY GCC	Saudi Arabia
REMITTANCES (USD MILLIONS)	6,343
REMITTANCES PERCENTAGE OF GDP	27.2%

In 2015, Nepal issued a 'Free Visa, Free Ticket' directive that aimed to remove the burden of recruitment fees on workers. The Nepal Association of Foreign Employment Agencies (NAFEA) pushed back hard against the policy and refused to co-operate. In August 2017, the government committee anoounced the scheme had failed.

1

BETTER LIVES, BETTING ON MIGRATION

AS OF 2011, THERE WERE OVER 700,000 Nepali workers in the Middle East, and this number has since risen, with 400,000 now living and working in Qatar alone. Nepal and the Philippines are amongst the countries most dependent on remittances. However, that coupled with a lack of proper governance renders Nepalese migrants extremely vulnerable, while in the Philippines it has given them a collective voice.

"They are lucky to have jobs here, because their life is better here than where they come from."

The dehumanisation of low-income migrant workers is often justified or brushed aside based on this argument. One part of that argument is partly true, the other is completely false. In fact, one cannot be farther off the mark.

When they migrate for better income, they also face isolation, discrimination, and harsh living and working environments.

Low-income Nepalese workers migrate to the Gulf because they earn more and their savings potential is higher. However, their life is not better. There is a broad line that separates economic needs (paying school fees, building a house, accumulating capital for a business) from quality of life (abundant supply of fresh produce, close knit families, supportive community, little houses nested in the Himalayan hills and valleys).

The life here is in stark contrast to the one lower-income migrants lead in the Gulf states. Home is community and well-being; a strong support system that doesn't isolate based on gender; a quality of life that is natural to the geo-location. When they migrate for better income, they also face isolation, discrimination, and harsh living and working environments. Which begs the question: does money equate wealth? The human capital deficit in the GCC is poverty of sorts, too. Yet, migrant workers continue to be dehumanised because there is little cognisance of what and whom workers leave behind to build the economies of countries that don't have enough manpower to be self-sufficient.

A lack of respect for that human capital both in cash-strapped countries of origin and flush countries of destination leads to desperation and exploitation.

"I had said I will never go abroad. But the situation is such now, I have no choice."

THE VILLAGE REMITTANCES BUILT

We drive three hours out of Kathmandu to the Tanahun district and pull up by the roadside. The car can't go any further. A 20-minute walk uphill leads to the village of Yampaphant. Single-roomed houses, many with corrugated roofs, nestle on the hill-face. Each has its own kitchen garden, cattle shed, and a tiny toilet. A tap by the garden serves as a wash area.

Some houses are brighter, bigger; some cattle sheds have more cows than others; a few homes also have a poultry farm. Affluence is determined by the livestock one owns. That affluence more often than not comes from remittances.

The milk is the tastiest I've had. The yoghurt is creamy and prepared daily. The cattle provide manure for the organic kitchen gardens, and fresh cauliflower and greens are sold to the middleman too. The food is so wholesome that one wonders how they could ever survive the onslaught of processed food they receive abroad.

At dawn, the dirt roads are busiest. Children in smart uniforms rush to catch the bus to the 'Montessori', a term used loosely to define private English medium schools. Fresh produce from the kitchen garden, eggs, poultry, and milk from cattle are taken to the middleman by the bus stop on the highway. The farmers are aware that what they receive is not even half of what the final market price will be. They have no other means of reaching the consumer.

The Nepali government has invested little in the entrepreneurial dreams of its citizens. Agriculture accounts for over 70% of its economic activities, yet farmlands are being abandoned for what are seen as lucrative offers in the GCC and Malaysia.

The Government does little to correct this.

Somprasad Lamichane and his family of returning migrants play host. His father spent several years in Doha in the 1990s; his brother spent a couple of years in Qatar too. Somprasad lived in Saudi Arabia for five years.

Though young, he is also the 'big brother'; the one the villagers turn to for advice on migration and contracts, on starting businesses and finding sustainable income once they return from their foreign employment. His is the story that most hopeful migrants aspire to.

But Yampaphant has some dire stories as well. Every household in this tiny village has someone working in the Gulf, or a returnee, or someone preparing to go.

Somprasad has managed to organise a cooperative of sorts for the cattle farmers, including his brother. About 10-12 of them sell milk collectively, ensuring better rates. Still, it's just one small step.

There are plans to expand the cooperative, setting up subsidiary cottage industries to produce dairy products. Even the best-laid plans need governmental and financial support, both of which are in short supply.

So labour migration is seen as the best course of action.

"First I wanted to do something in my country...I didn't succeed. So I will go to Bahrain, to improve my economic status."

WAITING FOR THE 'CALL'

Shriram Amgain (26) has a Bachelor's degree in Business Science. He is now going to Bahrain.

Shriram walks me through his village. Animated and full of plans, he says going abroad was not his Plan A.

"First I wanted to do something in my country, I started a poultry farm. But I didn't succeed. So I will go to Bahrain, to improve my economic status."

His words, entirely. He brushes off my attempts at speaking in Hindi, preferring to speak in English.

"Two months ago I went to Kathmandu to All Moon Overseas manpower company. The Bahrain factory required 42 people, there were 23 candidates in first round of interview, and only six were selected, I was one of them. Then a Skype interview with the company. Second round interview only I was selected. I will work as a service person in a restaurant."

"Do you know how the work environment will be?"

"They told me it won't be difficult work," a split-second flicker of doubt in his eyes, before he says: "Once I gain some knowledge about the hotel line, I can return and establish in my country."

He has paid NPR50500 (US$500) for medical evaluations and will pay another NPR100,000 (US$1000) once he receives the visa. All of this has been borrowed from family and friends in the village, in addition to debts he has already incurred.

"There's no facility here for business. When I did poultry farm, I lost a lot of money. The market price didn›t match our costs. Within two months I lost NPR200,000 (US$2000). I borrowed from family and friends in the community."

"Why not a bank loan?"

"I would have had to mortgage my property, I didn't want to do that. I am still paying interest on that loan." "Have you heard of the problems Nepalese face in the Gulf ?"

"Yes, my brother also warned me that life will not be easy there." Brother is Som, more a term of respect than consanguinity. "There is no opportunity for me here to earn that money."

That money being the cash he needs to pay off debts and build a business.

"I had said I will never go abroad. But the situation is such now, I have no choice. In my family there are 5 members. Parents, grandmother and sister. There is no other income source. My father was working in a paper mill, for many years. But the company shut down, and they didn't give two years salary. It's still pending, because they are in losses. So my father is back here and doing farming. But it's not good income."

He is upbeat. Foreign employment is the panacea to all his economic woes.

"I will be paid BD130 [NPR35000, US$350]. They will give me food and accommodation. Visa is for two years. I want to stay five years. Then I will have enough money to do something in my own country. I plan to save 30,000 every month, after expenses."

It seems cruel to point out that his savings estimate is way too ambitious. It seems more cruel to let him believe in it. I keep silent. So does Somprasad.

"Have you done your research on Bahrain?"

"At the time of interview, I did. I liked what I read about the country. Only after that I told them try Bahrain. First I tried Dubai because I have friends and family there. I was waiting for visa interview, but the agent said there was no job there now, and suggested Bahrain."

(At the time of publishing this book, Shriram had been to Bahrain and returned within two months because he was overworked and underpaid.)

We continue walking through small villages, through hilly roads and picturesque ponds, all looking out to the snow-topped mountain ranges. Som and Shriram take turns pointing out several brightly painted houses. "Remittance house." It's a refrain one hears a lot. Any sign of affluence has a remittance prefix. It's that prefix that is the carrot at the end of the stick.

2

RETURNEES' DREAMS. SOME INTERRUPTED.

WE TRAVERSE NARROW CULVERTS IN STEEP SLOPES to reach homes in deeper reaches of the hills. Sounds of running water and the smell of clean mountain air. Plump faced children in tattered clothes play under a large tree that serves as a village square.

We stop at Maneprasad's home. He returned to Yampaphant seven months ago, after a six-year stint in Saudi Arabia.

"I worked in a cafeteria in Abha. They promised me food and accommodation but didn't give me anything. Just my salary."

Maneprasad went to Saudi via India, a route taken by many to bypass the training and orientation required in formal migration. He is stoic about his Gulf experience. He makes a sweeping a gesture, to show what he built in the six years. A modest little home.

"What do you do now? Do you run a business?"

"Nothing. Just..."

"Do you share your experience with others?"

"I don't tell people anything. Don't ask them to go or not to go."

"...My best friend there, 26 years old, came back from a long day's duty and went to bed and never woke up. I couldn't stay there after that."

THE MANY SHADES OF RETURNEES

His reluctance to share his experiences is not unique either. Most returnees prefer to maintain an image of success and well-being, similar to what they aspired to pre-departure.

Ravindra Prasad is more vocal. He spent two years in Qatar and returned in 2011.

He shows his poultry shed. The radio blares 24x7. The music keeps the hens calm and prevents them from running wild. They have enough space to move, but not too much. Innovative free range poultry. He is proud of what he has here.

"I worked as a waiter in a bakery. The salary was too low, just 700 riyals [NPR19,000, US$190]. They gave accommodation but no food. I worked 11 hours daily, though contract said eight hours. Instead of three hours overtime we got only for one hour."

He says loud enough for the young aspirant by my side to hear.

"If I had worked this hard here, I would have made more money. This is what I tell people here in the village.

"I spent NPR100,000 [US$1000] to go there. Took a loan, and spent eight months paying it back, after which I saved for my business."

Ravindra doesn't mince words. "People don't want to work so hard here. I chose not to make my house, instead invested in business. It's a decision my wife and I took. My children ask me sometimes if I will go back to the Gulf, because they see others in the community. I will never go back.

"A lot of people just waste their time waiting for a 'foreign' opportunity."

And that's evident. Many returnees Migrant-Rights.org met have been back for several months and wait for the next opportunity. Not all see potential for sustenance working locally.

Somprasad, our host and a returning migrant, says: "People don't have long-term business plan. If there's a failure, they abandon.

"Then they go abroad for regular income. There is no support mechanism from the government to support businesses. So remigration happens all the time."

Ganga Prasad is amongst those seeking remigration.

His business ventures have not worked out as hoped, and he has no choice but to seek foreign employment yet again. He is a small, strong man with sinewy arms. He flips a heavy bench one-handed, and offers me a seat before setting out to share his story.

He ran away to India as a child and worked there for 15 years. As an adult, he worked in Qatar for seven years, five of which were at QAFCO (Qatar Fertiliser Company). He brings out all his documents and identity cards, carefully filed, including a recommendation letter.

"I worked for Professional Security Services. It's a supply company. So they didn't pay much. I paid NPR80,000 (USD 800) five years ago to get this job."

His initial QR800 salary increased to QR1,000 towards the end of the contract period. "But how can you save? Food is expensive, and you feel like eating good things. So not much chance to save a lot. Nepal is expensive, this is not enough to send home and family to survive and to save. But I continued making a little more with over time."

People doing similar work, directly employed by Qatar Petroleum, earned a lot more, he says.

"They would earn NPR200,000 or even 300,000 (USD 3000-2000). But as supplier, our pay and working conditions were bad. Too much pollution...fire, death."

"If I had worked this hard here (as in Qatar), I would have made more money. This is what I tell people here in the village."

Ganga worked 18 to 20 hours on average, with some shifts from 36-48 hours straight. "If your shift replacement didn't turn up you had to continue working. I couldn't leave my post. My salary would be cut."

Ganga took his employer to 'labour court' (the labour department) when they kept breaking their promise to send him on a long overdue vacation back home.

"They ruled in my favour. And company finally sent me. But they paid me very little. As per contract, I am supposed to earn 800 to 900 riyals basic, but even after overtime I would get only that much."

THE DEAD AND THE SURVIVING

It wasn't because of pay alone that he was desperate to leave Qatar.

"I wasn't feeling good. And then my best friend there, 26 years old, came back from a long day's duty and went to bed and never woke up. After that I wanted to leave. I couldn't stay there after that."

He reflects on why someone that young died. "Long work hours. It's very hot.

And we lived in a small room. Eight to twelve of us. You can never sleep well... one keeps waking up, one snores, one talks in his sleep. So you are sleepless most of the time. Maybe because of all this?"

Maybe.

Somprasad chips in. "See their lives here. There is hardly any motorised vehicles. There's no pollution. Their standards of hygiene is different too. Food and water is easily available here. And then they go there, and everything is different. They don't know how to cross the road or use the washrooms. They don't have proper food or water. Survival is difficult."

"Dilli Bahadur Kunwar died in Qatar a couple of years ago. He received no compensation from his employer, as he 'died in his sleep'."

A few days later, back in Kathmandu I meet Meena Kunwar and Bhavara Aiyari. Meena is in her 30s but looks much older; Bhavara is 18, but looks a child. The most valuable documents in their lives are in the worn-out backpacks they each carry. The death certificates of their respective husbands.

They have travelled a day and a half from the Salyan district of Nepal to claim compensation.

Dilli Bahadur Kunwar died in Qatar a couple of years ago. He received no compensation from his employer, as he 'died in his sleep'. He left behind his wife, son and four daughters. Nepal's Foreign Employment Promotion Board will pay them a compensation of NPR9000(USD900,000).

"I spoke to him on the morning of the fifth day of Dusshera (an important Hindu festival). We tried calling him again that night but couldn't reach him. His health was OK. He had been there only for seven months. And had sent back only NPR24000 in total. We paid NPR95000 as fees to the agent. So, with this compensation I have to pay all debts."

Next step for the family? Her 18-year-old son is seeking foreign employment. The cycle continues.

Bhavara's husband, Nar Bahadur Aiyari, went to Saudi Arabia and within three months was sent back due to poor health. Within a couple of weeks of return, he died. He was just 21.

"He was healthy when he went, the medical was clear. But on going there developed all kinds of issues," says his widow, who had been married for just six months.

"We need to see opportunities too. Not just problems."

POST-MORTEM GUESSES

Purna Bahardur Budha attempts to explain these deaths. A returning migrant himself, he is a social worker of sorts, helping families of migrants in his village.

"They work in the heat. Then they come home to air-conditioned atmosphere. When it becomes too cold. This has a toll on their health. Also there's not enough sleep. Then they die."

No one else seems to have a better explanation. Not even the doctors in Qatar who attribute these strange deaths of able-bodied young men to cardiac arrest. There's no arguing against the fact that lack of sleep, along with poor living and working conditions contribute to debilitating health.

Purna Bahadur is unable to work abroad again because of his health condition.

"In 2008 I went through a manpower agency to Qatar. I paid NPR95000. I worked for Hyundai directly. They paid on time. I worked for 19 months. But, I was promised 600 riyals, but was paid only 472 riyals. If I did the 24-hour shift five days a month, and 14 hours on regular days, then I would manage to get 1300 riyals with overtime. But it was difficult. Sleeping only for four to five hours."

Nirmala Thapa is the Director of the Secretariat of Foreign Employment Information Board. She tells Migrant-Rights.org that two to three bodies are being brought in daily. "We provide compensation and other support, but we can't do much in destination countries. They don't help."

That point that was raised during the Qatar Labor Minister's recent visit to Nepal.

The families of at least 70% of Nepali migrant workers who died in Qatar were deprived of compensation. In the past four years alone, 684 Nepali workers died in Qatar, according to the Foreign Employment Promotion Board. The Board had issued reimbursement to families of 205 deceased workers in 2013-14; 110 in 2012-13; 130 in 2011-12; 125 in 2010-11; and 114 in 2009-10, though the exact number of death is said to be higher.

Nirmala is quick to point out: "We need to see opportunities too. Not just problems."

Most players do see the opportunities, but returning migrants have more clarity about the challenges.

Dhal Singh Magar is also a returnee and works as a social worker and counsellor through Gefont. "I was in Qatar for five years with the Seashore manpower supply company. I worked two years in construction, one year in cargo ship, two years in a regular company."

He now counsels potential migrants, preparing them for what they should expect there. How receptive are the potential migrants? Do they listen?

"Not all of them. But many do. It's too hot. No proper water, and they end up drinking sugary fizzy drinks that make it worse. That really affects their health as they are not used to it. The worst part of Qatar is the accommodation, hundreds sharing just one or two bathrooms.

"We give better information than the orientation centre, including laws of destination countries, about contract substitution, etc. We also share details of existing contacts in the places they are going to."

Which brings us to the most reviled and unregulated part of the migration cycle: recruitment and orientation.

"We need to see opportunities too. Not just problems."

3

RECRUITMENT OR HUMAN TRAFFICKING?

IN THE VILLAGES, THERE IS A SAVIOUR and he is simply called 'agent'. He takes on the garb of the bogeyman in global migration narratives: the corrupt recruitment agent preying on gullible citizens and packing them off to hostile shores.

The truth lies between the two extremes. There has been little or no effort in streamlining recruitment agents in Nepal. Word on the streets is that the owners of the agencies are politically well-connected.

Countries of destination too often shirk their responsibility in curtailing trafficking. As far as they're concerned, it's a problem of and limited to sending countries.

KA-CHING! ECONOMICS TRUMPS HUMANITY

The reason recruitment agents have a free run is that about a fourth of Nepal's 19.4 billion dollar GDP is from remittances. According to the World Bank, in 2013, Nepal received USD5,551,527,542 in personal remittances. This is not accounting for money transfers through illegal channels.

Little wonder the country is reluctant to rock the boat and jeopardise manpower export. There is little monitoring of agents and training centres, and migration is so widespread that there are no mechanisms in place to reach out to remote parts of Nepal.

Laxman Basnet, General Secretary of South Asian Regional Trade Union Council, at a recent ILO event said 55% of households in Nepal were dependent on a migrant family member and their remittances.

This naturally takes the pressure off the government to provide for the citizens.

Yet, there's an opportunity to arrive at the same results by making the process cleaner and more ethical, without preventing citizens from migration.

"Most potential migrants don't know what a contract is, leave alone substitution or fake contract. they believe everything the agent says."

Somprasad Lamichane, a returning migrant, is a strong proponent of migration.

"They should go. Migration and remittances help us. But they should go with proper training and orientation."

He is one of the founders of the Pravasi Nepal Coordination Committee, which was conceived by five Nepali migrant workers in Saudi who saw a need for better education on safe migration. Among them, their wealth of lived experiences in both exploitation and success brings an insight absent from most other organisations run by 'experts.'

"The pre-departure training is not properly executed. Often they don't even get training, just a certificate. Teachers have no experience. They just talk. It's about how to go to airport, using toilet inside the aircraft, etc. Also environment of destination countries. But it's not categorised. Malaysia or Qatar or Saudi they all receive same training. In fact, they should receive orientation even before they get a passport. Not in the last moment before they leave the country. As it stands, during the orientation they are told not to pay agent without a receipt. This is futile. They arrive at training only after having gone through those processes."

Every day 4,000 applications for passports are submitted. It is at this point that orientation should take place, says Somprasad.

Jitendra Jonchhe of GEFONT (General Federation of Nepalese Trade Unions) has proof of how inefficient training centres are. He is on the recently set-up monitoring committee that tours districts to inspect training centres. There are 122 such centres in Nepal.

"Look at this photo." In this centre there were two potential migrants sitting in the room facing an overhead a screen with some notes on it. That's the training they will receive. Not even a trainer in the room.

GEFONT works with potential migrants and tries to educate them on safe migration. In their team are people like Dhal Bahadur who are returning migrants with far more knowledge than the trainers at the centre.

But this is not always easy. GEFONT is a trade union. According to Gopal Ghimre, the potential migrants don't want to listen to trade unions. "They are brainwashed by recruitment agents. They've been warned not to interact with unions, as they would lose their opportunities."

Somprasad says in the decade since his own migration journey, very little has changed. "There is no awareness. I was not aware eight years ago. They are not aware even now. Most potential migrants don't know what a contract is, leave alone substitution or fake contract. They believe everything the agent says. About 60% are illiterate and they don't know what's written. Once they reach destination countries, they are surprised. Their expectations are so high."

"They [Qatar] are strict, so agents don't charge much commission. in the UAE for instance, they encourage workers to pay a portion of the migration costs."

THE BUSINESS OF RECRUITMENT

Uddav Shrestha is the director of Energy Overseas Manpower Company, which, according to him, is a small-scale agency and should not be targeted.

He is nostalgic for an era – a decade ago – when there were fewer manpower agents and enough profits to ensure there wasn't so much corruption.

"A decade ago, employers used to come and recruit directly. Now they prefer doing it through their local agency. We could also contact companies through yellow pages and ask them for requirements. Then employer would come here directly the first time, and be involved in the process. Once they trust us, we take care of interviews and placements.

"At the beginning, there were just 10 to 20 agents. Now there are almost 1000 registered agents. Earlier, workers would pay a meagre fee, employer would bear costs and by mobilising just a thousand workers a year the company could make profits, making USD 300-400 per person. We were happy."

Uddav says when companies in destination realised this was good money making business "they started local manpower agencies there. They take [fees] from employer and from us."

In his analysis, the problem of fees lies with manpower agencies in countries of destination, and the problem of exploitation with employers.

"Employer manipulates the job demand data. They might have more than one company and shift workers around. So both job and salary will be different from what give here in the contract. Sometimes workers are homesick or ill and we can manage that. Not the first."

Costs of migration is dependent on receiving countries.

"Qatar is an exception. They are strict, so agents don't charge much commission. The worker is not supposed to pay for visa or ticket."

He doesn't see a problem if workers have to. "In the UAE for instance, they encourage workers to pay a portion of the migration costs. Say 40% of the visa fee and your joining ticket. Their logic is if you contribute to costs then you have invested in the company and will be loyal and will not run away. This is the company securing its interests. On completion of contract they would provide return ticket."

He refuses to be nailed down on overcharging workers. "It would be very fortunate if employer pays for everything. The NPR70000 workers pay us, which is legal, it covers all expenses including passport, tickets etc. Within that our margin is also there. Most manpower companies are satisfied with USD 100-150 per person. We have to make money, no? Manpower agencies in the Gulf don't pay anything."

"Some workers accuse agents of overcharging more than the stipulated NPR 80,000 over 100,000 even?"

"This is off-track question... when they pay that much, I assure you it's not manpower agency eating the 150k. We are satisfied with much less. That much is charged to make sure it's good companies. It's related to demand and supply..."

RECRUITMENT AGENTS ARE PASSPORT TRADERS

Dr. Gurung, from the Nepal Institute of Development Studies, believes that the migration narrative should shift from victimisation to empowerment, because that is closest to the truth.

"We just finished a financial literacy programme for families of migrants, linking this with how to save money. Important to involve spouses at the household level. There are informal systems of remittances – hawala etc – and we want them to do it in proper channels. The guess is 40% comes in through illegal channels."

Dr. Gurung also sees remittances as a tool to counter effects of climate change, especially in an agro-centric economy. "This money is used to adapt to a newly created environment."

He says it's no longer about creating jobs, since that has failed. The unemployment rate in 2008 was over 40%.

"It's about creating value chain, tapping into their current economic activity. Something practically beneficial for the families. For instance, producing and selling milk, they would get minimum profit. But if they work on processes and products, their profits would rise. Create cooperative and sell directly, doing away with middlemen and brokers."

Some groups do attempt to do so informally, as we have discussed here.

Dr. Gurung also underlines the importance of social remittances, that often goes unacknowledged.

NO INVESTMENT IN RETURNEES

"We only focus on financial remittance. We don't talk about skill, knowledge and experience, because they are exposed to different environment, they are mature. They are right for entrepreneurship. This has to be capitalised.

"People focus on negative aspects only. But the number adversely affected is small... we need to focus on what can be gained." In his assessment, the Nepalese government is not focusing on opportunities with returnees.

"There is no enabling environment for returning migrants. No schemes. General fatalistic perception, nothing can be done here, so 90% want to go back as migrants."

Even with those going abroad, 70% are unskilled as Nepal hasn't assessed labour markets in receiving countries – a process essential to matching up worker skills.

"Of course, we can't only send semi-skilled and skilled, unskilled lose opportunities. There's a need for them as well. Need a combination. This has to be packaged."

He comes down hard on recruitment agents and dubs them 'passport traders.'

"There are 1,035 recruitment companies registered, of which 600 to 700 are operational. Only one is known as ethical. And they are all based in Kathmandu, due to regulations."

This centralisation has given room for unregulated manpower trade in rural Nepal.

Dr. Gurung places equal blame on donors and NGOs for staying silent in the face of corrupt recruitment practices.

"The donors, in the absence of strong civil society, should play a stronger role. And they are failing. In their silence, they are compliant."

GOVERNMENT TO GOVERNMENT RECRUITMENT AS AN OPTION

Cleaning up and introducing better practices in recruitment is an urgent need.

The EPS with South Korea, which is a government-to-government (G-to-G) system, has resulted in much less exploitation. "Recruitment agents are obviously unhappy with this. Destination countries, especially in the GCC, should invest in our country. Be active in our training centres. Set the curriculum. Tap into our potential.

"Engage directly with us. Meet families. Meet recruiters. Try and understand the environment."

In return, Dr. Gurung says, these countries that are so dependent on foreign labour will get mentally well-prepared workers, increasing efficiency.

"This is also a way of loosening the stranglehold middlemen have over migration and migrants. Help households improve. Now the system enriches brokers, not workers. The gap between haves and have-nots is increasing."

*"They should go. Migration and remittances help us.
But they should go with proper training and orientation."*

*"I did everything. It was a two-story house,
so I had to wake up at 5 a.m. and would be done by 11 p.m."*

INDONESIA

Published July-August 2015

POPULATION	266,486,980
NUMBER OF MIGRANTS IN THE GCC	630,000–1,000,000
MAIN RECEIVING COUNTRY GLOBAL	Malayasia
MAIN RECEIVING COUNTRY GCC	Saudi Arabia
REMITTANCES (USD MILLIONS)	8,663
REMITTANCES PERCENTAGE OF GDP	0.8%

In 2015, Indonesia banned deployment of female workers to 21 countries, most of them in the Middle East. Many migrant workers, particularly domestic workers, still travel to the region through irregular channels."

4

COMMODIFICATION OF WOMEN IN RURAL INDONESIA

SADIYA (29) SITS IN A CORNER, HER hijab draped differently from the norm in Indonesia. She is seen as a successful migrant. After four years in Saudi Arabia, she has managed to buy land and return for good. And she had made two million Indonesian Rupiah by merely agreeing to work in Saudi.

Hers is the story and dream that drives young women to migrate for work. A belief that short-term overseas employment is a panacea; to come back and build their dreams on sacrifices made thousands of miles away. Between that brink of hope, leap of faith and reality, many dreams splinter.

THE WOMEN

Like most other migrant domestic workers (MDWs) in her Karawang district village, her migration plan was short-term. Leaving behind young children, her plan was to return as soon as set goals were met.

"My Arabi (Arab employer) were very good. They paid me on time." She had to care for five children, three of whom were disabled. Sadiya says she was happy while there and with what she achieved.

With trepidation, we discuss the details of her employment.

"How many maids?"

"Just me."

She hesitates before continuing.

"I did everything. It was a two-story house, so I had to wake up at 5 a.m. and would be done by 11 p.m."

"You sent money every month?"

"No. Every five or six months. I got 800 riyals monthly, so will save up and send. They promised an increase after two years, but I didn't get."

"Did you go for Hajj?"

"No. But they promised me."

She straightens her back. "I went for Umrah twice. So I am happy."

"What did you do during your free time? You called your family?"

"I was very lonely," she says, rubbing her chest repeatedly.

"I had no phone. No friends. No off day. When they were not at home I would watch T.V. I couldn't otherwise. And if I wanted to speak to my family, I had to use their phone. I slept on the carpet, on the floor of the children's room. I missed my daughter a lot, she was just four years old when I left her."

"Do you advise other women about migrating and working?"

"There's no need. People will do what they have to. I did."

There is a resignation, acceptance of terms, condoning the lack of rights in degrees. It could be worse.

For instance, Kartini. Her mother, Darasih, awaits her return. "She hasn't called for so long. And hasn't sent money either." Kartini went to Saudi five years ago; after the first two years, contact dwindled.

"Where in Saudi?"

"We don't know. She didn't tell us."

"Has the agency helped?"

"No. That agency was blacklisted and already shut down."

Kartini had remitted money a few times, but that too stopped. "She wanted to leave her employer, and they put her in another house. Since then we haven't heard from her. In between, once she called from her friend's phone. We could not even inform her when her father died. And she hasn't even received her salary in three years," the mother weeps.

As we sit listening to the ageing mother, neighbours convene, occupying empty spots on rickety benches, shooing away a straying hen and its line of chicks.

They listen with curiosity but not surprise. In a village full of migrants, these stories are common.

Karawang, West Java, where Migrant-Rights.org spent a day, there used to be a major supplier of domestic workers to Saudi. Both religion and economics play a role in encouraging migration.

Families are paid money to seal the contract and the women are recruited. Saudi in particular, and the GCC in general, are seen as a good place to work for young Muslim women, despite evidence to the contrary.

Employment in Saudi also comes with an anticipation of doing Hajj. Many employers offer this in the contract and many deliver on the promise. This is a journey which would be out of reach for most impoverished Indonesians.

The irony that the Hajj so conducted is not recognised by the Indonesian Hajj board is lost on the workers and their families.

Engkas, who stands at the threshold of Darasih's home, smiles and insists her migration was good. She had only two stints, and secured her family's future. She suggests measures to help Kartini. The family looks at her with suspicion. "Are you undermining our worries?"

"No, I've been there twice and made a good life. And I know how the system works..." she walks away, not wanting to squabble.

Another neighbor, Itham, stares at her, sucking on a rolled tobacco. "My wife is in Abu Dhabi. She sends money. But no contact. A man answers her phone when I call. I will give you her number, call her when you go back to Arab."

Everyone has an 'Arabia' story.

Agents pay the family a signing fee to lure the women into employment in the gulf. Once that's done, then the designated worker has little choice but to migrate.

THE CHALO

In a tiny village of a few dozen households, names of Gulf towns roll of their tongues with ease, with nostalgia and often with a sigh. And the Chalo (registered recruitment agent) is an important man in the community.

Chalo Omo Wijaya lounges in his sofa. His home is a concrete structure, more whole than other houses in the area. There is a motorcycle and a small garden. Obvious affluence. He has been in the trade since 2000.

Over the doorway, inside his sitting room are three frames – a place of honour next to a tapestry rendition of the Ka'aba.

One frame holds the photo of the couple, one is his agent's certificate and square in the middle is a photo with the owner of the agency from 'Arab Saudi.'

This man has been responsible for Omo's prosperity. "Past prosperity," he says, with a flick of his hand.

He harks back to a time when regulations were not so strict, and he could charge hefty recruitment fees. "There's too much competition now. Too many Chalos."

Omo brings out a register from a locked cupboard. Page after page of mug shots of women he helped migrate. There's one page that looks like an account statement. Recorded neatly on that page is what Omo received from the families, and what was still due of families who chose to pay a percentage of the monthly salary instead of a lump sum. They often sold property or took loans at steep interests to pay for a job in the Middle East. This page of accounts ends abruptly, because in recent years the trend has changed.

Agents now pay the family a fee – a signing fee – to lure the women into employment in the Gulf. Once the family takes the money, it's as good as spent. Once that's done, then the designated worker has little choice but to migrate.

Some workers we spoke to say this money is returned to the Chalo over the period of employment. Some others say it's a bonus that they don't have to return. There are no set rules to the game; the goal is one: Get as many women, preferably young, to the Gulf to work as domestic workers.

The register, dog-eared and bloated with images and age, is proof of lives Omo has improved, his wife, Narmi, reminds us.

She is a returning migrant herself, and encourages young women to seek opportunities in the Gulf to better the lot of their families. Her life has improved substantially; her children are married and settled into their own families.

Despite the level of comfort, Omo is not a happy man. He stares out into the large plantain leaves swishing in the rain, and says, "No one wants to go to Arab. The government doesn't want anyone to go. And those who manage to, it's all through the young Chalos who don't do it legally."

"Do you advise other women about migrating and working?"
"There's no need. People will do what they have to. I did."

5

RECRUITED UNDER DURESS, UNTRAINED AND UNPREPARED FOR MIGRATION

IN AN INCREASINGLY UNFAVOURABLE MIGRATION ENVIRONMENT, FAMILIES in rural Indonesia have to be lured into sending their young women to the Middle East. Thousands of unregistered sub-agents scout villages for vulnerable and willing families. These sub-agents or field officers work under the radar, while chalos (like Omo, whom we met in our previous chapter) are registered with the government.

Following interviews with families and returning migrants, we stop for tea at the home of Dadang Muchtar, the chairperson of Karawang Migrant Workers' Solidarity Center. He has gathered a group of 'field officers' (sub-agents), returning migrants (including Sadiya), and families of migrants. His home is in the Paserkaliki village in the Karawang district.

THE BAN THAT ISN'T

While the group is well aware of the risks migrants face, they don't agree with the moratoriums and bans the Indonesian government puts in place. "This just puts them (migrants) at greater risk. And how do you provide employment to all these people, if you don't allow them to seek opportunities abroad?"

Dadang has never worked abroad, but many of his family members do, including his sister. He speaks favourably of migration, and works with the community on safe migration. "Lives can change when people go abroad and work. There's not much job opportunities in Karawang. Local industries and agriculture doesn't pay much."

It's not government policies alone that inhibit migration now. "People now want to go for vocational training. They are looking at self-development. Which is good. But ultimately, when they want to start their own business or buy land, they have no choice [but to migrate]."

"The domestic workers are not trained in a particular skill [...] however, employers in the receiving countries are looking for and are promised workers with specific skills."

He deduces that, despite the ban on new migration to Saudi, many go via Oman or Abu Dhabi. Wadi, who is part of the assembled group, says his wife is in a training center, getting ready to go to Qatar.

"There's a ban. How will she go?"

"She has a visa for another Arab country too. But she will work in Qatar."

"Who told you?"

"The chalo. And the training center."

Marna, a sub-agent, chips in. "The numbers have reduced, but people still go. There's no real ban."

His work covers 14 villages in Karawang, and he deploys workers to various agencies, getting Rupiah 4 million (about USD 300) per worker. "I keep 1.2 million for myself. Rest to the family."

The chalo and the sub-agents are the ones held accountable by the community and the first person to be 'punished' when something goes wrong.

"Do you receive complaints from workers in the Middle East?"

"Yes, mainly about salary. And I tell the [manpower] agency. But we get little help."

Once a domestic worker leaves Indonesia, the responsibility is scattered across various governmental and private agencies across both countries, and no one is held accountable when there's a problem.

Dadang recalls the case of the Indonesian maid, Nani Suryani, who was murdered in January 2011 by her 'madam.' "We didn't get the body till February 2012. And the family received no blood money. The governments' response on both sides was inconsistent."

Still, women go under duress. "Families compel them to go. To pay off existing debts. To build homes or businesses. Then it gets worse. Many men end up marrying again when the wife is away. They continue to receive and use the remittance. And they have also received that signing fee."

The chalos receive about Rupiah 10 million per worker (USD 750) from the recruitment agency. They keep half of this, and distribute the rest between sub-agents and the families of potential migrant workers. With that, the family is held in a sort of bondage. The young woman is shipped off to Jakarta, to one of the training centers.

They will surrender their mobile phones, and not have any contact with the outside world during the training period.

40 DAYS OF NON-TRAINING

The training centers are all in Jakarta. From Indonesia, there are two main routes of labour migration: one to the Asia-Pacific and the other to the Middle East.

The profiles of domestic workers (maids) going these two different routes is a study in contrasts. So is the nature of training.

We visit a couple of training centers. One is stuck in a time warp, with twilight lighting and in-your-face Western Union posters. The other is all marble and water fountain, and seems like a students' hostel, except for the high 'prison' gates.

As we drive out of a large bungalow, a van full of potential workers is brought in. They enter the place that will host them for six to seven weeks of training and paperwork before they are deemed fit to be shipped off to countries in the Gulf.

This new vanload of young women will join the 100 others inside who are at different stages of training. They will surrender their mobile phones, and not have any contact with the outside world during the training period. And on every wall is a Western Union sponsored poster. But that's a story for a different day (Indonesia receives USD 8.4 billion in remittances annually).

This center deals exclusively with recruitment to the GCC. The manager, Pheri, insisted that none were going to Qatar or Saudi, and that the majority were headed to Abu Dhabi and Oman.

At the time of the visit, Indonesia had placed a ban on workers going to Saudi Arabia and Qatar alone. It has since extended it to 17 countries, including all GCC states. However, this doesn't deter workers from coming to the Gulf through il-legal routes.

Pheri says there are two kinds of workers that they train. Formal – cleaning services, hospitality; and domestic workers – maids, nannies, cooks.

The latter train for 40 days, 10 hours a day. All their paperwork, from passports to visas to medical, is the responsibility of his agency. The chalos in the village only scout for potential workers, the rest is taken care of by the training center.

The domestic workers are not trained in a particular skill. "We just push them towards what they are good at," he says.

However, employers in the receiving countries are looking for and are prom-ised (by local recruitment agencies) workers with specific skills. Quite clearly, there is many a slip between cup and lip. With regular prayer breaks, the trainees go through the motions of pushing prams and setting tables for hours on end. They look bored.

The bungalow that houses the training center is decorated on the lines of an imagined Arab home. Faded and worn-out furniture, that probably was considered luxury in the distant past, is neatly arranged. There's the bedroom with a dressing table; a nursery with a pram, toys and changing table; sitting staidly in the middle of this chaos is a dining table set for a four-course meal; a laundry area; and a kitchen with museum pieces of appliances. Then there's a majlis with a sheesha as a centerpiece. Yes, they will be training to set up and ready a sheesha too.

Beyond the 'Arab' home set-up, is the backyard turned into a dining area for the ladies. A few trainees on the benches exchange a whispered words and look into what appears as a surreal preview of the life that awaits them a few thousand miles away.

The trainer knows this is not ideal.

"This is the government prescribed training material, we know none of this will be there in the Gulf and everything is new. When they go there everything will be different," says the trainer.

Pheri says learning Arabic is compulsory and 80%of the returnees (those who have worked in the GCC previously) speak it well. All the trainees are Muslims and are in hijab, in the age group of 21 to 38 years. Formal workers are in the 18 to 30 age group. These are the boxes that they are ticking off to make their trainees ap-pealing to potential employers.

As a first step, the family of the worker needs to give permission, and the vil-

lage head has to give a letter. The willingness of the worker herself is assumed, and never questioned.

RELUCTANT RECRUITS

On the first floor of the bungalow is a large hallway where prayers are held and sermons given. Lining the hallway are the dorms. On the grilled stairwell sit a group of women looking down into the drawing room where we are seated. The air is thick with what I could only describe as tension. It could just as well be mugginess, given the overcrowding and humidity.

We manage hurried conversations with a few of them before the designated interviewees meet us. The informal chats reveal that many are still going to the countries Indonesia has placed a ban on.

Officially, new migration to Saudi has been banned since 2011, and to Qatar since 2014.

Migration to Abu Dhabi and Oman have been on the rise, though, and the agents use that as a transit point before sending them to Saudi or Qatar. The checkpoints are only at the Jakarta departure terminal. Once clear of that, these bans hold no meaning.

A community worker says the trade in passports is quite high too. The ban doesn't apply for returning migrants. So once you return after your stint, you could pledge your passport for a commission, and someone else would travel on that.

The players in the chain of exploitative migration are many, with the worker herself having little or no say.

As a first step, the family of the worker needs to give permission, and the village head has to give a letter. The willingness of the worker herself is assumed, and never questioned. Once training is completed, four stakeholders sign the employment contract: the Indonesian Embassy, the Bureau of Migrant Workers, the director of the agency in Indonesia and the director of the agency in the receiving country. There are two other contracts: between the agencies in Indonesia and in the Gulf; and between the employer and agency in the Gulf country. Again, the employee's acceptance is implied. Not explicit.

The trainer brings in two trainees. The older of the two, Lisnawati (38) worked in Dammam, Saudi Arabia, between 2006 and 2009. She is the one who speaks 'fluent' Arabic. I quiz her, and her pidgin Arabic makes me sound like a scholar. "I don't remember anything," she giggles.

Her three-year stint with a family of 16 (including 12 children) helped her build a home for her family.

"They were good. I woke up at 4 a.m. to prepare breakfast. Once they left to work and school I could sleep a little again. Then I worked again from 9 a.m. to 11 p.m. When the children were home they helped me, because I was the only maid."

She sent back home all of the 800 riyals they paid her monthly. "I was allowed to use their phone to call home and they took care of my other needs. And I didn't need much. I didn't have an off day and went out with them. Even to Hajj. So I didn't need money."

Six years after her return, she prepares to go back. This time to support her husband's business dream. "He is a driver still, and wants to run his own taxi company."

The six million rupiah the agency paid her to go to Saudi has already been spent.

Twenty two-year-old Ratnawati is more reticent. She is leaving behind her four-year-old son to go to Bahrain and earn money to build a home. She doesn't know where Bahrain is. "The returnees have given me some dos and don'ts. Yes, I am scared, but what to do? I have to build a house."

"Do you know who your employer is?"

"No. How?" She looks perplexed.

A small number of them do Skype with potential employers. The rest of them enter employment and migration blindly. To Pheri, that's normal.

"What if there's a problem when they land?"

"They contact the agency here or there. Main complaint is salary. They are promised Omani Riyal 120 or Qatari Riyal 1200 and don't receive it there."

"What about the isolation they face. Do you give them phone numbers or contact of other maids whom you have placed in those countries?"

"No. Why should we? That's dangerous." He doesn't explain why it's dangerous.

"We have to motivate the workers to go to the middle east. Keep giving them hope. Because they anticipate more trouble."

ASIA-PACIFIC, AHOY!

The next training center we enter is large and airy. But for the giant, double-layered prison-like gates, one could easily mistake this center for a students' hostel. A good one at that. The training center itself is a modern building with a central courtyard and a fountain.

The financial burden of migrant recruitment is almost entirely borne by the employer, in the case of the GCC. Asia-Pacific migration places the burden on the workers. However, the workers are paid much more, are more empowered, and have more freedom in those countries. Each group chooses the sacrifices and compromises they are willing to make.

Asramaputri has worked as a trainer for over a decade, and has trained thousands of workers headed to the Middle East and Asia-Pacific region.

"These are two distinct profiles. To the Middle East they go mainly as helpers. The madam is home most of the time, so the maid just helps. To Asia-Pacific they have to be more independent. Employers are never home, and often it's for elderly or child care."

Accordingly, the training differs. So does the tone of training. "We have to motivate the workers to go to the Middle East. Keep giving them hope. Because they anticipate more trouble. Whereas, for Asia-Pacific, we just have to talk to them about financial literacy and all that. They are already motivated. They have freedom there, and they get paid more."

Monthly salaries can go up to USD 3000 in Taiwan and Hong Kong, especially for elderly care. They also pay a hefty recruitment fees. Up to 50% of their monthly salary is deducted at source by the employer to pay the agent.

Niken, who works for the Shelter Me project, surveys domestic workers at the airport, pre-departure. She notices a similar trend. "The ones going to the Middle East are not aware and look scared. Especially the new migrants. They cling to the one or two returnees in the group. However, those going to Asia-Pacific are well-spoken and seem more empowered. It's very stark."

Since there is no ban on formal workers, many domestic workers go on that visa, and end up working in private households, she says.

With governments of employment and origin refusing to talk or cooperate with each other, there is enough scope for blurry avenues of employment. Countries in the GCC are under no mandate to recognise Indonesia's ban. They then absolve themselves of all responsibility for how the worker was recruited.

As Indonesia insists there's a ban in place, it sees little or no need to build resources in its mission to deal with problems that might arise. In a situation that is lose-lose, each party maintains that it has done its best to protect migrant workers.

"…it is hard to spot an able-bodied man.
The few you see are either home on vacation or waiting to migrate."

INDIA

Published July –August 2016 (Tamil Nadu)
and May–June 2018 (Uttar Pradesh)

POPULATION	1.3 billion
NUMBER OF MIGRANTS IN THE GCC	7,216,365
MAIN RECEIVING COUNTRY GLOBAL	Saudi Arabia
MAIN RECEIVING COUNTRY GCC	Saudi Arabia
REMITTANCES (USD MILLIONS)	69,000
REMITTANCES PERCENTAGE OF GDP	2.7%

Recruitment of prospective workers who have not passed grade 10 (ECR passport) holders must (legally) take place through the e-migrate system, a platform which digitalises interactions between the employer, recruitment agent and potential employee.

6

INDIAN FISHERMEN: BETWEEN THE DEVIL AND THE DEEP SEA

"IT'S A VILLAGE FULL OF TOOTHLESS AND useless men," Father Churchill says, only half joking. The former are the aged, and the latter are the children.

The picturesque coastal village of Muttom in India's southernmost district Kanyakumari is unlike other fishing villages. No huts on the beach; no catamarans lining the shore; not even the smell of fish, just a salty breeze cutting through the humid summer days.

Concrete houses vie with each other to boast of successful forays the men have made to fish in the waters of the Arabian and Persian Gulf. These are deep sea fishermen used to spending weeks away from shore. Neither their families nor they quite know if the sea gods will allow them safe return.

Father Churchill of the South Asian Fishermen Federation and his colleagues work closely with the community in this district, both to help those in distress and to empower those who remain.

A majority of the people in these areas have embraced Christianity, and juxtapose onto their new faith the superstitions and beliefs of their previous dogma. So the goddess who protects them while at sea and decides their fate is a Biblical figure in a white saree.

The houses are colourful with small doorways on narrow streets and large open windows facing the expansive Indian Ocean. The hospitality is overwhelming. Every home greets us with sugary tea and cakes.

"We can't fear the sea; life or death, our fate is indelibly linked to the salt of the ocean," Ritammal shrugs. And that sea knows no boundary for her four sons in the Gulf, and the rest of the coastal families.

So while they fret and worry when their men are at sea, be it in the Indian Ocean or the Arabian sea, they know no other life, nor wish to seek another.

As you walk through the tiny fishing hamlets in the southernmost areas of India, it is hard to spot an able-bodied man. The few you see are either home on vacation or waiting to migrate.

It's the women, children (the useless), and the aged (the toothless) who greet you, eager to share stories and photos of their menfolk, and allow you a peek into the relative prosperity remittances afford.

DECEPTIVE AFFLUENCE

So you see streets of affluent-looking homes, many far grander than what the owner could actually afford. In debt, and drowning in multiple mortgages, the men keep returning to the harbours of the GCC.

The vagaries of the seas are the least of the migrant fishermen's concerns. Rather, it's being arrested by the coast guards of Iran or the GCC states. Over the last decade, thousands of fishermen have been detained and made to pay hefty penalties.

Yet, they are not deterred from migration.

In the last 13 years, Ritammal has seen four of her sons move to Saudi. Her house reflects it. On a corner plot of land stands a three- storeyed concrete house. Colourful, and furnished with every household luxury one could imagine.

"The pirates and the coast guards are both a problem," says Ritammal, echoing what others we interview say. They speak of the officials and the robbers as one. "We can be detained, robbed, or killed by any of them and no one will question it."

Lissy's husband Edward has been working in Saudi for the last 10 years, for the same sponsor. "The kafeel is a good man, but the risks are high at sea. The pirates come and take whatever they can from the boat, and sometimes even beat them up. But he hasn't been arrested..." she pauses, "...yet."

Ritammal's youngest son is home from Saudi on vacation. He insists on not being named or photographed. "I have to go back to Dhahran and I don't want my kafeel to get upset," he murmurs.

"We are paid every two months, the kafeel gives us a share of our catch. This is not much. Some kafeels take up to 60%. And fish stock is dwindling. Trade has declined drastically."

So, would it be better to stay behind in India?

His mother offers the reason, collectively for her sons and the rest of migrant workers in the fishing industry. "The salt of the sea is our life. We can't do work on the shore."

Fish stock off the Indian coast has been dwindling for decades, and the state has not invested enough in protecting the trade or the fish workers.

As Father Churchill points out, there just aren't enough landing centres. There is just the one private harbour in Muttom, where fishermen in mechanised boats bring in their catch and trade.

On the street that Ritammal lives, almost every house has someone working in the Gulf. So stories of hardship in foreign seas are common.

Vinoj for instance, has worked in Saudi Arabia for 15 years. "People do come and ask him for advice," says his wife Bonslee. "They are aware of problems there... but always the hope that things will get better. Once you've decided then you can't really stop."

The ones who can't make a living off the Indian coast may attempt shore work, according to the women we meet. But it's not something that they are happy doing. 'Shore work' is a broad term for anything that's not to do with the sea.

ARRESTS AND DETENTION

As we walk away from Ritammal's house, Helena, who is my guide for the day, says the fishermen will go where there's fish. Intrinsically they don't recognise the borders. "They are all under great pressure to get a big catch, and hope every time that this once, the sea gods will help us get away."

Rubin, Helena's husband, went to Ajman in May 2015. A 'captain' in the village arranged for his visa. The captain is the one who recruits his crew here, usually from amongst his family and friends. The captain usually receives a recruitment fee.

"He tried to fish here. We don't have facilities for nets, for docking... it was a struggle. Nearly six months in a year there will be no work, and we go into debt. Rest of the time, they might make a profit of Rs 500 a week, sometimes Rs 2000. There's no assurance."

Rubin was amongst the 49 fishermen caught crossing waters from UAE to Iran.

From those 49, 8 fishermen were from Muttom alone.

Subeida receives us with a stack of papers. Home loan documents, a copy of her her husband Seelan's passport, and her daughter's mark sheets. On the day we meet, Seelan and his colleagues have just been released after being detained in Qatar for three months.

Seelan has been working in Saudi Arabia for 19 years. And this is not the first time he has been caught crossing borders.

"This time was different. They hadn't crossed the border. The coast guards told them they just had some questions and urged them to cross. And then arrested them. They didn't this time."

She hazards a guess, "I think the guards who catch them get promotions."

"The sponsor paid Saudi Riyal 5000 for each crew member as fine. Now they have to pay back the sponsor and can't come back till then."

The three months in Qatar, and the next few months paying off the fine, means the family goes deeper into debt. "My daughter is a very good student. She goes to an English medium school. It's time to pay school fees. And the house loan too... we can't quite manage. But banks will give a loan only based on their foreign employment, even if we would never earn enough to comfortably pay back."

Her voice is strong and belies the tears streaming down her cheeks.

It appears that at any given point of time, in this village alone, a family or two would be awaiting news of an arrested family member.

*"We can be detained, robbed, or killed by any of them
and no one will question it."*

7

LIFE AFTER ARRESTS

IN 2014, SASHIKUMAR AND HIS CREW WERE detained by Iran when their Qatar-licensed boat crossed the border. For three months they were stranded on the Kish island. Migrant-Rights.org advocated for their release and helped repatriate them.

After 10 weeks of detention and uncertainty across two countries, five Indian fishermen finally left Qatar on Wednesday, Novemeber 26.

In a tiny room that houses eight, in Wakrah—a coastal town bordering Doha, the fishermen spoke to Migrant-Rights.org about the nightmare that began at sea and continued on land in Qatar. First they were caught in cross-border politics, and then in the shackles of the kafala system that immobilised them in Qatar.

It's been 18 months since Sashikumar's release when we sit down with his wife, Sheela, in a tiny house down a narrow street lined with stacks of drying fish. When we last spoke to Sashikumar, just after his release, he and Sheela were expecting their first child.

A teary-eyed Sheela explains the stress of those months resulted in a stillbirth. "After 10 years I finally got pregnant... and then."

Sashi's story is not a strange one for the village. He first went to Qatar 20 years ago to secure a future for his family: to get his sisters married first, and then to set up his own family.

Sakunthala, of the NGO National Domestic Workers Federation (NDWF), works with the families of fish workers. She says the women of the community were all highly educated, unlike the men. Yet, they preferred to marry within the community. Huge dowries are doled out by the women, and the men in turn promise a lifestyle that they can ill afford.

Father Churchill agrees. "These men who stay out for long periods of time indulge their wives, build comfortable homes; the few days they are on shore they want to experience luxury that offsets their trials in the rough seas."

That's just one minor reason why 60% of men in the Kanyakumari district migrate, Sakunthala says. "Only then [when they migrate] is there any economic development. They have to fend for themselves, as the government provides no support. Fishing yields just Rs150 to 200 per day. From there [the GCC], they can send upto Rs30,000 to 40,000 a month. Good season even Rs100,000."

Yet, there is very little awareness. "They don't even carry passport copy with them. Families don't have copies of their paper. When they are arrested on land in trouble it's a struggle to get paperwork done." Currently, the NDWF is conducting a campaign to educate fishermen and their families on this.

There are also attempts now to impart financial literacy to prevent fishermen from being trapped into circular migration just to pay off debts.

Sheela, a seamstress, supplements the family income. Would she prefer it if Sashi stayed back in India?

"He is traumatised. He owned a boat and was deep sea fishing when it broke and no one helped him. Finally as he clung to a raft, fighting for his life, a merchant navy ship rescued him. He is scared now to go to these seas," she waves towards the ocean that we can hear but not see, beyond the walls of her house.

"Wait, I will give him a missed call and he will call back. He wants to talk to you. Ask him."

The phone rings soon enough. An Iran number flashes across the screen. Months after he returned, in February 2015, he went abroad again, this time to Iran. A gentleman helped him when they were detained onin Kish island, and offered him a job.

KISH, A RESORT AND A JAIL

"It's a 'super' island," laughs Benjamin.

He was one of the Ajman detainees. His wife fills in the gaps of his narration, every time he pauses to shake his head, as if to say 'never again.'

He migrated to the Gulf only in July 2015 after paying Rs 35,000. He recounts the trauma they set sail to on November 15.

"There were five boats, mine was owned by a Sharjah sponsor. We worked in Ajman. Other four had an Ajman kafeel. We used to go near Iran border often, because the kafeel gets angry by our low catch, and would push us.

"We were all anchored in an island off UAE coast due to high winds. During that time, the captain of one of the other boats told us that his kafeel had paid the coast guards. So we all went into Iranian waters. That's where the trade is really good. Good harvest of fish," he says, and explains how the crew functions at sea.

The captain remains on the boat. Every boat has about three rafts. The crew usually get on the rafts, with their nets, to look for a catch. Once they get a good enough catch, the nets are pulled onto the boat. The captain and the crew communicate on wireless.

On December 1 they set out to fish.

"Our captain contacted us on the wireless and told us they were caught. He asked us to cut the nets and run away. The coast guard managed to catch up. They caught 49 of us then. We were on eight boats. Three escaped."

So the coast guards were not bribed?

"I don't think it's true that the CG was bribed. It was more to encourage us to go without fear."

For three long months he and his compatriots survived on bare rations, living on their boats anchored off Kish island.

"When fishermen go missing, the government doesn't even know until we write to them."

UNNECESSARY CRIMINALISATION

Given the geopolitics of the Gulf region, fishermen being arrested is never just about crossing borders.

"During this time, an Iran launch was caught within the UAE. Iran negotiated, asking UAE to release that boat in exchange for the five boats we were on. Dubai said nothing could be done as this was a ganja case. We were told we couldn't depend on negotiation and sought the help of the embassy through Sister Valarmathi [of NDWF]."

On March 3, he and the 48 other Indians were repatriated.

Sister Valarmathi's rough estimate is that around 70 to 80 fishermen have been arrested so far in 2016 alone, of whom about 10 to 15 still await release or resolution.

Father Churchill bemoans the lack of influence Indian embassies have in the countries of destination. "How can workers land in a country and the embassy there not even be aware? When fishermen go missing, the government doesn't even know until we write to them. When fishermen are arrested or detained in neighbouring countries, it is not reported to Indian authorities. Captain doesn't want to inform them. They prefer going to the sponsor directly. Neither they [the Embassy] respect Indians, nor are they respected by others."

He also feels strongly that fishermen, even if they cross borders, should not be criminalised. "And when you do find a fisherman violating your borders, you need to have a speedy trial. They cannot afford to be arrested and without an earning for weeks and months, as they don't receive a set salary."

He understands that the GCC states and Iran wish to guard their stock either for conservation or economic reasons, and hence suggests: "Countries in the GCC need to have a treaty on this, on the lines of IOTC, which will extend some protection to fishermen."

He also feels that the Indian government should be involved in the treaty in some capacity because its citizens are in the crosshairs.

Benjamin says they can't go to work depending on the 'Dubai' seas alone. The problem is, even if the catch is good in Iran, the economy isn't. Everyone comes to the UAE to sell the fish.

"We didn't realise the risks before going to Dubai. Having gone there, we had no choice but to work at all costs. The travel agents play the role of recruitment agents and send people without any proper training."

He accepts that each person has a different experience. The more seasoned kafeels with larger fleets have better practices, he says.

"Would you like to go back?"

"No. I don't even have a passport. Only the white passport," he holds up the emergency, bleached version of the blue Indian passport.

"Only then [when they migrate] is there any economic development.
They have to fend for themselves, as the government provides no support.

8

HIGH SKILLS, LOW VALUE: INDIFFERENT GOVERNMENTS ON BOTH ENDS OF MIGRATION

A STONE'S THROW AWAY FROM THE ONLY LANDING centre in Muttam (a private one at that) is a modest concrete building. In a bright, airy, sparsely-furnished room is a metal cupboard filled to the brim with folders. Each contains a plea to officials and history of the fishermen's journey from Kanyakumari to incarceration in a Gulf state or Iran. Some of these files are of fishermen who are being held to ransom by their sponsors.

The letters written by South Asian Fishermen's Federation are uniform in tone and structure. Sheets of passport-sized mugshots, with personal details and an explainer.

Scenario one: The fishermen are caught crossing borders and detained. The Indian embassies in both country of employment and destination are presented with details of the case and asked to help pay the fine and secure the fishermen's release.

Scenario two: The fishermen have been going to sea for months, and the sponsor does not pay them for their share of their catch. After about six months and sometimes even a year, the fishermen refuse to go to sea, and demand to be returned to their home countries. The sponsor refuses to issue an exit permit. The embassy's help is sought to secure the permit.

Every family in Muttam has a story, and the ones that don't have one answer every overseas call with dread. Or worse still, when they don't hear from their men, they borrow other people's stories to fill the gaps.

Yet, as soon as a boy turns 18, he heads to one of a handful of travel agents in Nagercoil, the closest town. As important as the kith or kin who would secure a job for them in the Gulf is the local travel agent, who will help them acquire a passport and process immigration papers.

TSUNAMI EFFECT?

Sakuntala of the National Domestic Workers Federation, who helps us meet families in Muttam, says a lot of lives were lost during the tsunami. "Garbage was being washed ashore. Quite a few of the fishermen were scared to go back. So there was skills training for shore-based jobs. But not enough opportunities in that either. So more migration. Fishing also reduced."

Kadiapattinam is a village neighbouring Muttom, and was hit hard post-tsunami. "There are 1,500 families, all of them with a family member in the Gulf. About 500 in Qatar and the rest in Saudi."

Father Churchill, on the other hand, doesn't feel the tsunami affected migration as much. "It just pushed people to an alternative way of living. In the last 20 years, every family has two to three [migrants abroad]. Earlier, a [whole] village had only 2 or 3. They used to invest only in the sea. Tsunami changed that. They wanted to invest in land, too. Earlier they either lived on church land or government plots."

He lists a cocktail of reasons, most of which are to do with the local government's indifference, that escalate migration.

"As a fisherman here, your earnings are not cumulative. It's meagre, and the family spends it for sustenance. More importantly, in Tamil Nadu we don't have sufficient graft (equipment) or landing centres. Even for the graft that the fishermen have, there isn't sufficient instruments like harbours and fish landing centres."

This is the sorry state of affairs despite fishing being the mainstay of the community. The Kanyakumari district accounts for a third of all fishermen in the state of Tamil Nadu. "All are active fishermen here. Neighbouring Kerala has many more fish landing centres, even though they don't have as many fishermen."

The caste-based politics of India extends quite deep into Tamil Nadu, and explicitly impacts fishermen.

"The state is politically governed. So the community [caste] that has political representation will have their needs met by the government. The last time any investment was made in the fishing industry was in 1962, when mechanised boats were introduced. That, too, because the fisheries minister was from the community."

There are about 300,000 fishermen in Kanyakumari district alone. Of them, 100,000 are active, and 50,000 have migrated – nearly 25,000 fishermen to the Gulf alone.

Furthermore, because of extensive trawling the fish source has depleted drastically.

Trawling remains a contentious issue between Sri Lanka and India, but neither has been able to quell the problem.

The Indian boats, most of them owned by rich Tamil Nadu businessmen with strong political connections, have trespassed into Sri Lankan waters for several decades, ravaging the seabed with their heavy trawls.

So much so that Sri Lanka, desperate to keep a check on Indian fishermen, is considering limited licences. A Sri Lankan weekly reports:

Fisheries Minister Mahinda Amaraweera said the Defence Secretary had mentioned the proposal. "It has been put forward as an idea and it is not necessarily a bad one," he explained. "At present, 2,000 to 3,000 Indian trawlers fish in our waters. The aim is to reduce this to about 250 and to issue licences to them. But we must first speak to our people, especially our fisher associations. If they agree, we will implement it."

"They've erased the source of fishing. It is banned by the state, but people still do so. Because no alternatives are given," explains Father Churchill.

In Qatar as well, mechanised bottom trawlers were permitted. "When it caused trouble for the oil pipelines, they bought the graft and net and gave their citizens subsidies for other kinds of fishing," he says, comparing it to the Indian government, which has not given an alternative. "So they go ahead with available methods."

A WHOLE LOAD OF PAPERWORK, BUT NO CONTRACT

The week we visit Muttam is at the end of what the Tamils call 'Modaku', a two-month rest period for fish stock to replenish. Benjamin says this is the law of the sea, but the Gulf has introduced this only belatedly, after they felt the pinch of dwindling stock. Each coast has a different period allocated for this.

So there are a few fishermen home on leave in Muttam. And they speak of Mangalam travels as much as they do about the 'Kafeel' or 'Arabi'. In a bustling junction near the local administrative offices is a dingy four-storeyed building. On the second floor is Mangalam travels, a well-lit contrast to the drab exteriors.

Robin, a client servicing executive, spoke to us about the role of the agency in helping fishermen migrate.

"The visas are usually brought by the captain or the driver who works with the sponsor. For each country, the process is different. And whatever costs the fishermen pays for. They first do their medical that costs about Rs2000. Almost 90% go to Saudi Arabia. Those headed to Qatar come with a readymade visa. Saudi and Kuwait visa has to be stamped pre-departure and is facilitated by registered agencies in Mumbai. We help with that. Then we book tickets. Bahrain and Oman, only medical has to be done pre-departure."

For every component there is a fee, and the total could be as low as Rs10,000 (US$149) covering tickets alone, or as high as Rs50,000 (US$750) that covers all the paperwork. This does not include amounts paid to the 'captain' as a recruitment fee.

At no point in this process is a contract in play.

They work without minimum wages, end of service benefits, a recognised contract or any kind of financial support.

Shaja, who we met earlier in the series is well-versed in the ways of the Gulf. Her husband Ravikumar has worked in the Gulf for several years, first in Saudi and now in Dubai.

"They are encouraged by their kafeels to cross the seas, and the kafeel would bail them out. But they have to pay him back. My husband had to pay back Rs100,000 [US$1,490] to the kafeel when he was caught and released by Iran in 2013."

One part of what the fishermen earn is theirs. "Usually the captain gets two shares, kafeel and rest get one share of catch. Sometimes the kafeel gets the majority share and rest shared by crew."

First the UAE, and now the rest of the Gulf states, have set a five-day limit on the length of time the boat can be out at sea, to prevent overfishing. This reduces significantly the number of fishing days, and correspondingly, the number of earning days. And in those five days, they are encouraged to push their luck and violate boundaries.

"In the fishing line, sponsors are completely dependent on fishermen. So they won't sign a contract. They can't afford to pay if there's been no catch," says Robin, matter-of-factly.

He says about 90% of their business is dependent on fishermen. They come with visas sent by people they trust. We help with processes. In a month 40-50 fishermen come to this agency alone, to get tickets and other paperwork done.

"A lot of people come back cheated." And there is no contract that they can hold to account.

THE SHACKLES OF KAFALA

The fishermen are neither covered by the e-migrate system of India, nor the labor laws of countries of employment. They work in an unregulated vacuum, subject to the vagaries of commercial interests, climate change and blinkered governance.

In the GCC, domestic workers are classified as those who work in private households as cooks, nannies, caretakers, gardeners, drivers. The fishermen, with their seaman's visas, are excluded from the labor laws and fall under the purview of domestic workers immigration management.

"The fishing community in Kanyakumari are adventurous. These are the only deep sea fishermen who migrate, even globally. They can stay up to 50 days at sea. So these men are sought after as they are good fishermen and adventurous. The Arab sponsors seek these fishermen out," says Father Churchill.

These sponsors, however, are not fishermen. They invest in the sea solely dependent on migrants to run the risky business. They find a captain, who then builds his crew. The captain is the one who communicates with sponsor on needs. He then puts out a call in his village, and each fish worker then pays the captain anywhere between Rs100,000 to 300,000, he says.

If things sour between sponsor and fishermen, then they are trapped in the kafala system, with little or no access to legal recourse.

"Fishermen turn 18 and they get a passport and can't wait to fly abroad. There is no pre-departure training as the Indian government doesn't care. Neither does the Gulf. It is bonded labor there, even if they recognise the value of these fishermen."

The fishermen survive on 'advance' and 'running accounts' in local grocery stores, as their share is not paid immediately. Even that share is disputed.

"They will know how much they catch, but they don't know what it yields. It's what the kafeel says it is."

He recounts the case of 63 fishermen on 15 boats in Jubail, Saudi Arabia. "All owned by the Amiri Al Khalidhi company. They were not given their share of fishing for seven months. Last two months they have been asking to to return. Sponsor has refused, as he would be investigated if 63 of his sponsored employees leave all at once. And he would be unable to get more visas. Yet, he won't pay the share."

Once the fishermen land in the Gulf, their passports are confiscated, and all that they have on them is a seaman's identity card.

For these men who spend days at sea, and months in seclusion away from their families, faith is a cornerstone of survival. Even that is under threat.

"For fishermen, their religion and faith is very important. And they can't even carry any Christian iconography. For personal freedom, Qatar is better. They can practise their religion in the privacy of their homes. In Saudi they are attacked.

"They are away from country, family and culture. All they have left is their faith, and you take that away from them. They can see God through symbols. You want their labour for your economy, but you can't allow them their right to life."

"A lot of people come back cheated."
And there is no contract that they can hold to account.

9

MIGRATION IN THE TIMES OF DISTRUST

SAUDI ARABIA, BECAUSE OF ISLAM, AND DUBAI, because of its glitz, have always been a draw for migrants from Uttar Pradesh. But it was nowhere close to the numbers one saw from the southern parts of India, particularly Kerala.

That trend is now changing due to a combination of factors: dwindling livelihoods, real and perceived socio-economic insecurity, and an ever-stronger underground recruitment network. Migration is not discouraged, and the government is trying to weld together its skills development, national employment and migration strategies.

Janakipuram is an area on the outskirts of the capital city, Lucknow, which is also known as the city of Nawabs. Lucknow was a key outpost in both Mughal and British India, the vestiges of which are still visible. Recent investments have ensured a fairly good infrastructure, too.

Janakipuram is a contrast. A short diversion from the crowded market areas and the highway, you enter a time warp – a grid of dirt roads, lined mainly with mud homes, and a moat of open drain.

Children, goats, and poultry alike roll around in the dirt. It takes a while to process the din – the uncontrolled giggles of the children, the competing bleating, and the disembodied chatter of young women from behind doorways and curtains.

You see a few women on the streets – the old and the young with children old enough to give them the liberty of being publicly visibly. The rest are mostly young children, boys and men.

AN ART, BUT NOT A LIVELIHOOD

The women are busy with their embroidery (zari and zardosi work) and dyeing of stoles. Some men are working on the stretcher bars – large, locally devised embroidery frames - while others have set up their sewing machines under the shades of trees in the community courtyards.

The community refers humbly to their collective vocation as tailoring. What they do is more than stitching together pieces of fabric. It's art. Intricate needlework, silver relief on different kinds of fabric, stories in thread. Every front room has these frames, and children as young as six or seven start working on it.

It's a tradition and a habit, but no longer a livelihood. For that, the community has to seek seasonal work in neighbouring agricultural plots or migrate abroad.

Abdul Aziz's trajectory was slightly better to begin with. He was a driver in government service and is now a pensioner. Much of his savings were lost when his 24-year-old son Saddam Hussein tried migrating.

Fadrunissa is the most vocal in the family. She has seen both her husband's savings and her son's dreams disappear.

About seven months ago, an agent from Aliganj, Lucknow, came with a proposal. For a sum of money, he would get Saddam to Saudi Arabia. Saddam had completed a computer course and hoped to be employed as a computer operator.

"He (the agent) first took Rs10,000, then 50,000, then 15,000... and I spent a lot of money buying him (Saddam) clothes, toiletries to take with him," says Fadrunissa.

Abdul Aziz walks up to the corner of the crossroad where chairs have been pulled up on a flattened part of the mud road. "He (Rafiq) was his relative," she says, pointing to her husband.

GHOST OF AGENTS PAST AND PRESENT

A neighbour, Mohammed Arif, chips in. "Rafiq took money from a lot of people in this community. They dangle dreams in front of these people like lollipop to a child."

Abdul Aziz shrugs. "He has cheated 17 people, we hear. What to do? First when I called him, he kept making excuses. Now Rafiq doesn't even answer my phone calls. My son hasn't even seen his passport."

"I have seen a copy," Saddam says in a faint whisper, breaking his stoicness.

He has lost interest in going abroad now, worried he would land in the wrong job.

"Definitely will not send him to Saudi... maybe Dubai," his mother says hopefully, as Saddam walks away.

Afsar Jahan takes the just vacated seat. Her 'piya' (beloved) is in Jeddah, working as a driver.

The 45-year-old does not say his name. "Shakeel Ahmed," another neighbour offers, as Afsar giggles. In this community, there is no personal business; everyone has an opinion on everyone's affairs.

So while gaps are eagerly filled, it's a patchwork quilt, with loosely knotted ends and frayed edges.

Someone urges her to talk about Shakeel's first stint abroad.

"He went first in 2016, but came back in eight months. The kafeel was horrible. He was working as a driver in a home. He just waited to make a little money, because we had to pay Rs100,000 that time. Then again, five months ago, he went. This time he paid only 70,000."

Afsar and Shakeel have four daughters and one son, and though their family, like the rest in the community, were into zari work, it's no longer lucrative.

"He started driving... what can we do, there's no money in zari work."

That's the refrain in this area. Some take up driving, many go to Saudi and UAE to work as tailors and embroiders in small or home businesses.

It's the beginning of summer and vegetable vendors ferry carts of cucumbers. Some have it salted, some have it plain. Crowds gather around the card, goats in tow. Everyone knows that people are being interviewed about their Gulf experience. Everyone wants theirs heard.

"Saudi is not the same," one says.

A few others nod in agreement.

"It was becoming too liberal," another adds.

The conservative ethos they were familiar and comfortable with is waning.

"Women are going to drive there," one notes with disapproval.

And also a note of fear, as that would eat into the livelihoods of many of the men who go there as drivers, making mobility possible for the women there.

SEW, DRIVE, BUT GO COME WHAT MAY

Mohammed Salman was the driver of the taxi hired for a day. Slight of build and garrulous, the 24-year-old eavesdrops on the conversation and interjects. He boasts of his exploits when he worked as a driver in different households in the Gulf and provides his unsolicited advice to everyone we interview on the day.

"I spent 18 months in Saudi and 13 months in Dubai. But what's the use? So many pretty women, and you can't even look at them. Just stay in India." He would repeat this often – a bait and a warning rolled into one – to the googly-eyed youngsters eager to go to 'Jeddah' – a catchall name for anywhere in the Gulf.

Mohammed Abid chomps on a stick of cucumber. "I have my passport ready, I will go for Umrah and if I like it will stay on."

He doesn't know when that would be. "Need money, no? All people have money problem."

Musharaf Ali, who was casually listening in, agrees. He is a certified painter and he went to Jeddah last year. "I stayed for eight months. They put me to work as a construction worker, doing masonry. They didn't even pay me what was promised. It was supposed to be 1500 riyals and I got only 1200 riyals."

So he did what a lot of workers who are cheated do. "I escaped from my kafeel and went to another. But the police caught me."

On this street, Rafiq's name gives way to Raees. "I paid him 85,000. Pappu (pointing in the general direction of the group around the cucumber cart) also went through Raees. He is a zari worker, but they made him do construction work. What's the point in fighting [with the agent], everyone is struggling."

Musharaf would like to go back to Saudi, "but I have a five-year ban now."

CLOSE-KNIT BUT NOT CO-OPERATIVE

Barabanki is just an hour's drive from Lucknow city. The famous Dewa Dargah is the pride of the district. Bareti village is not far from the dargah.

An elder in the community, Sarfudin sits at his sewing machine in the shade of a tree outside his mud home.

Every home in this village also has a frame and hands on deck. He lends an ear to the woes of his community, but holds back from offering any big advice. There's a daily struggle to make ends meet; a growing inclination to go away; and an increasing frustration with the agents.

The dyeing and fringe-knotting of shawls, for instance, fetches just a rupee per piece. That's 1 cent. The final product sells for anything between USD 5 to as much as USD 50 in the international market.

For zari work, the rates differ, based on the intricacy of the work. But in a good week, the earnings are no more than Rs1,000 (USD14) per family. When it's a bad week, which it is more often than not, earnings are nil to 300.

It would probably make sense to organize a co-operative, so when work orders come in from the towns and cities, the rates could be negotiated better. Often the competition for that order is a race to the bottom.

Sarfudin thinks a while, and shakes his head. This is not a new idea.

"Each family does their own. No one trusts the other. Someone might cheat... So each family looks for its own order."

But agents are trusted with large sums of money despite mounting evidence against them.

A group of children hang around, curious about this strange mix of people – some with questions and one (Salman the taxi driver) with stories aplenty.

WHEN EDUCATION IS A CASUALTY

The children are multi-skilled. At five or six years of age they start learning the zari work. And at harvest time, they are out in the fields with their family, earning a daily wage cutting wheat crop. School and education are not priorities.

One of the older children says the schools are no good after primary, and that the teachers are not committed. So they might as well drop out and earn some money.

Some disagree, and blame families for not keeping children in school. "My wife is a teacher and she has to beg the students to come to school. But parents know an extra pair of hands in this (harvest) season would fetch good money."

Alok Pandey and Sanjay Sharma are grassroots social workers with Grameen Development Services who try to educate these communities on safe migration. "The general feeling we get is that they see no hope here. They all have large families with just one or two people working. In fact, the pradhan (head) of Sirori village was complaining that families pull children as young as 10 and 12 out of schools and make them work. Because that means Rs3,000 more a month."

Education is not seen as an escape from poverty. Especially when families keep growing, the older children have no choice but to drop out and work.

Uttar Pradesh (UP) is India's most highly populated state and its fourth largest in area. It is also one of the poorest in the country. According to a recent study, while India's ranking has improved in the Multidimensional Poverty Index*, this improvement was largely due to southern states, with those like UP where 31% of the population are classed as multidimensional poor, continuing to flounder .

Throw into this mix the fact that UP is the single largest sender of migrants in the ECR category. ECR (Emigration Check Required) passport holders are those who do not have a high school leaving certificate, and hence are considered unskilled and are often employed in lower income jobs.

None of this information bodes well for the most socially and economically marginalised communities within the state – the Muslims and the dalits who constitute close to 40% of the population.

Increasingly, cross-border migration is seen as the only alternative to escaping dire poverty because there's no trust in federal instruments that promise jobs and development.

"My wife is a teacher and she has to beg the students to come to school. But parents know an extra pair of hands in this (harvest) season would fetch good money."

10

OF BOGEYMEN AND WILLING PREY

IN VILLAGE AFTER VILLAGE, HOME AFTER HOME, it's the same story: a community of shared distress and deja vu; and no one fighting back or holding accountable the agents who are painted in shades of black and grey.

Noor Allam went to Jeddah when he was just 19, in 2005. He went on an Umrah visa and stayed on irregularly for four years.

"I was doing zari work for a Yemeni's workshop... he said he was Saudi. I got 1200 riyals and the work hours was long. I would have stayed on, but got caught by the police and I am now blacklisted."

He tried going to Dubai, again irregularly, and his passport was damaged.

"Now I want to go to Qatar," he says, holding up his entry visa. He didn't have much time at that point to pay the agent the final amount. "I have paid 40,000 to Asif (the agent) already, and now have to pay another 45,000."

Noor, like the rest of the people we speak to, has little awareness of what the regular migration process looks like, or any interest in finding out more about it, as they don't trust the government or the system.

The reason, in theory at least, is that a neighbour or relative who is an 'agent' can be held more accountable than an office in a strange town. Even if the agent often takes no responsibility. Like when Abdul Wahabi's brother Mohammed Tayif returned from Mecca after three months, having endured severe hardships without food or money. The agent, 150,000 rupees richer thanks to Tayif, shrugged it off by saying, "It's your kismet, what can I do."

Tayif was supposed to do zari work in a home business, but ended up doing household work for an abusive kafeel, and fought to come back. Now he has a five-year ban slapped on him, and his wife has lost all the jewellery pledged to raise recruitment charges.

THE STORIES, REPETITIVE; THE HARDSHIPS, UNIFORM.

They refuse to believe that you can migrate without getting into debt. Justifiably so... while on paper that's a possibility, the sheer size of the country, the extreme poverty of the state they come from, and the marginalisation (both forced and self-inflicted) make it impossible to navigate the system without falling prey to false promises and fraudulent agents.

Buddhu and Amina have four sons. Sacks of onions and other fresh produce are stacked up on one side of the verandah that leads to their home. The family buys vegetables wholesale from the nearest town and retail it in their small village. It's barely enough to make ends meet.

They still managed to muster more than Rs200,000 to send one son to Dubai and the other to Kuwait. Both earned less than expected and the latter was subject to abuse and ill-treatment by the 'madam' of the house where he works as a driver.

Yet, there's no two ways about where the sons would rather work. "Everyone in the 'mohalla' (community) goes to Dubai or Jeddah."

As we sit on the raised verandah of Amina's home, many from the 'mohalla' drop in to offer their stories.

The storytelling is abruptly interrupted as a young man from the neighbourhood walks up to Amina's home and demands an identity card. "Anyone can print a business card. How do we know who you are? How can we trust you?"

We could well be the government poking its nose where it doesn't belong, he insinuates, adding as an afterthought, 'or an agent'.

Amina apologetically offers the 'best sweets from Mumbai' to make up for what she saw as an inhospitable interruption.

A short drive from there, in Gadi village, Nisar Alam and his mother are trying to make a plan for their future. The 21-year-old went to Ras Al Khaimah with the promise of a job in a juice shop.

His mother is beside herself. "I paid Rs85,000. He was supposed to make more (money)... pay that back, get his sisters married"

Nisar says he did know till he reached the Lucknow airport that he was going to the UAE on a tourist visa. Taju, the agent, had shared no information with him until that point.

"There was one more person with me at the airport. Same story. When we reached Ras Al Khaimah we were kept in a room. The agent took everything from us."

"Even the sweets I sent him... it went bad," the mother chips in.

Nisar and the other person shared a room with Taju's brother and his friends. "Taju's brother works there. He was supposed to find a job. And we had to pay for all our food. I only had 100dhs with me. I would get one roti and eat it over two days."

The family fought with the agent and made sure he paid for Nisar's ticket back, and he returned in less than a month. The rest of the money, according to Taju, went into expenses and cannot be returned.

Nisar's mother had borrowed money from neighbours, and is overwhelmed with the laundry list of problems in front of her. "I have to pay them back. I have to get two daughters married. And Nisar... what will happen to him?"

IN DEFENSE OF THE 'AGENT'

She is inconsolable, and her neighbours see it. Yet, another thirty or so went to the UAE with Taju's 'help' in the last few months – all on tourist visas and with the promise of a non-existent job.

Many were now being returned.

Taju's phone number is on everyone's contact list.

A quick call and a quicker dismissal of the problem follows.

"I have nothing to do with all this. Alika Travels (in Lucknow) gives visa and contract, I only help those I know well. I don't make money. He (Nisar) didn't want to work. It's not my problem. My brother also went on a tourist visa nearly two years ago, and he is employed and makes money. He does zari work. Nisar could have worked, he didn't want to," Taju says, over a phone call. "I paid for my brother, too. 70,000. How else can you go abroad. These people..."

Mohammed Imran has some sympathy for Taju and his likes.

Imran lives is Seepahiya village, and has a brick home and runs a small grocery store. Relative affluence in an otherwise decrepit street.

"You can't blame the agent. Everyone knows very well how they are going, what visa... it's common knowledge. Agents are not 'cheating'."

According to him, when someone doesn't like the job or are frightened in the new place, they say the agent cheated.

"He (the agent) takes money because that is his business. You go because you want to earn more money and you know the risks. There's one guy here (in his village) complaining about being a shepherd. But that's his visa, no? I met so many in Saudi too, who came like this."

Shan E Ilahi agrees with some of this argument. There are close to 300 unregistered agents in UP alone, he estimates.

Shan runs a travel agency in a crowded market, in the heart of Lucknow. His office is tucked away behind a row of shops selling colourful embroidered suits and sarees. He used to send workers regularly to Saudi and UAE, but now is waiting for registration of his business as per new regulations. Meanwhile, he provides travel services for tourism and pilgrimage.

"A local candidate will trust a local agent even if they are unlicensed. I am paying a lot to be registered, still the workers will go through those middlemen who mislead them. The workers going from UP are all unskilled and uneducated."

This is probably why even those who eventually reach out to a registered agent have to go through an illegal one. And probably why the government-run UP Financial Corporation, which also does overseas recruitment, has not to date made a single placement.

Shan is entrenched in both the community that migrates and the network that helps migration. And now he is the person a cheated returnee or potential migrant goes to.

On his desk is a tall pile of folders: cases he has helped register at various police stations, seeking justice for those taken for a ride by the rogue agents.

This doesn't make him particularly popular, as it disrupts an established business model, so cases are filed against him as well. "None of which has been proven," his father, a thus-far silent observer, says proudly.

THE DIRTY UNDERBELLY

The irregular migration process demands the cunning and ingenuity of many.

Saudi now is clamping down on those who overstay the Hajj and Umrah visa, and the agent is blacklisted. A new obstacle means a new innovation in smuggling and trafficking.

Shan explains what's common knowledge in the market: those with an ECR passport cannot exit the country without going through the due process.

"But here's the catch, the visa has to be stamped by the Saudi embassy here, but employer doesn't have to attest the contract with the Indian embassy. So there are chemicals that are used to remove this visa carefully, and workers are sent to Dubai on a tourist visa. In Dubai the Saudi visa is stuck back on the passport."

At every step there's a possibility for exposure and penalisation. Of the worker, not the agent.

Imran is something of an expert on the irregular migration process. He lays bare the workings of the migration underbelly, especially in Saudi, where the sheer size of the country allows people to hide in plain sight of the law.

He went to Saudi in 2011 on a tourist visa. "Fully aware... the free visa was too expensive, and this was only Rs65,000. Tailoring and embroidery workshops are really popular in Saudi, so I found a job and stayed for 22 months. I wanted to go and stay as long as possible. When they announced the amnesty in 2013, I came back."

The first year he was an unpaid apprentice, with food and lodging covered. "The following year, I could earn even 1200 riyals a month if there was good orders. There's an Indian businessman from Sitapur who runs his empire there in Saudi. The kafeel had visas that he distributed to smaller businesses. In the unit I worked in there were 20 of us. Not even one on a proper visa. None of us were paid monthly salary. We could get 50 riyals one day, 200 another, and nothing at all some days."

THE 'HUNDI'

Because of the haphazard payments and the lack of documents, the workers were all dependent on the 'hundi' or 'hawala' system. It's a hugely popular way of moving money, especially in the South Asian communities, and one that the government pushes back hard against.

There are no official currency conversion rates, promissory notes, or receipts, just trust and fervent prayers.

"When I had enough riyals I would go to a broker. He will say this amounts to 20,000 or 30,000 rupees and that's all... They would say day after we will give it to your family in Bareti or Seepahiya or whatever the village is. We will call our family. And as promised someone will be at the doorstep, with the money, on the promised day."

Imran thinks he might have sent 100,000 or 115,000 but is not sure how much he lost in conversion and fees.

"The hundi-wallahs (brokers) work out of small rooms all over the country (Saudi). All day, everyday, they just sit there collecting money from people working there. He has a network all over Uttar Pradesh too. "

Most of those who use this service may be undocumented workers. But there are also those whose families may be illiterate, don't know how to go to Western Union or a bank, and feel this is simpler.

"Everyone knows about the hundi there, just as they know about all the illegal workers in the sweatshops. An open secret that officials turn a blind eye to."

When the amnesty was announced, Imran escaped from his room and surrendered.

His post-migration plans did not pan out, and he wants to go back.

"Agent says if I have a high school certificate then I can get an ECNR (Emigration Check Not Required) passport. Easier to go then. I will wait and go the proper way. Other people's experience does not matter. You have to be hit bad and experience all that yourself before you change your methods."

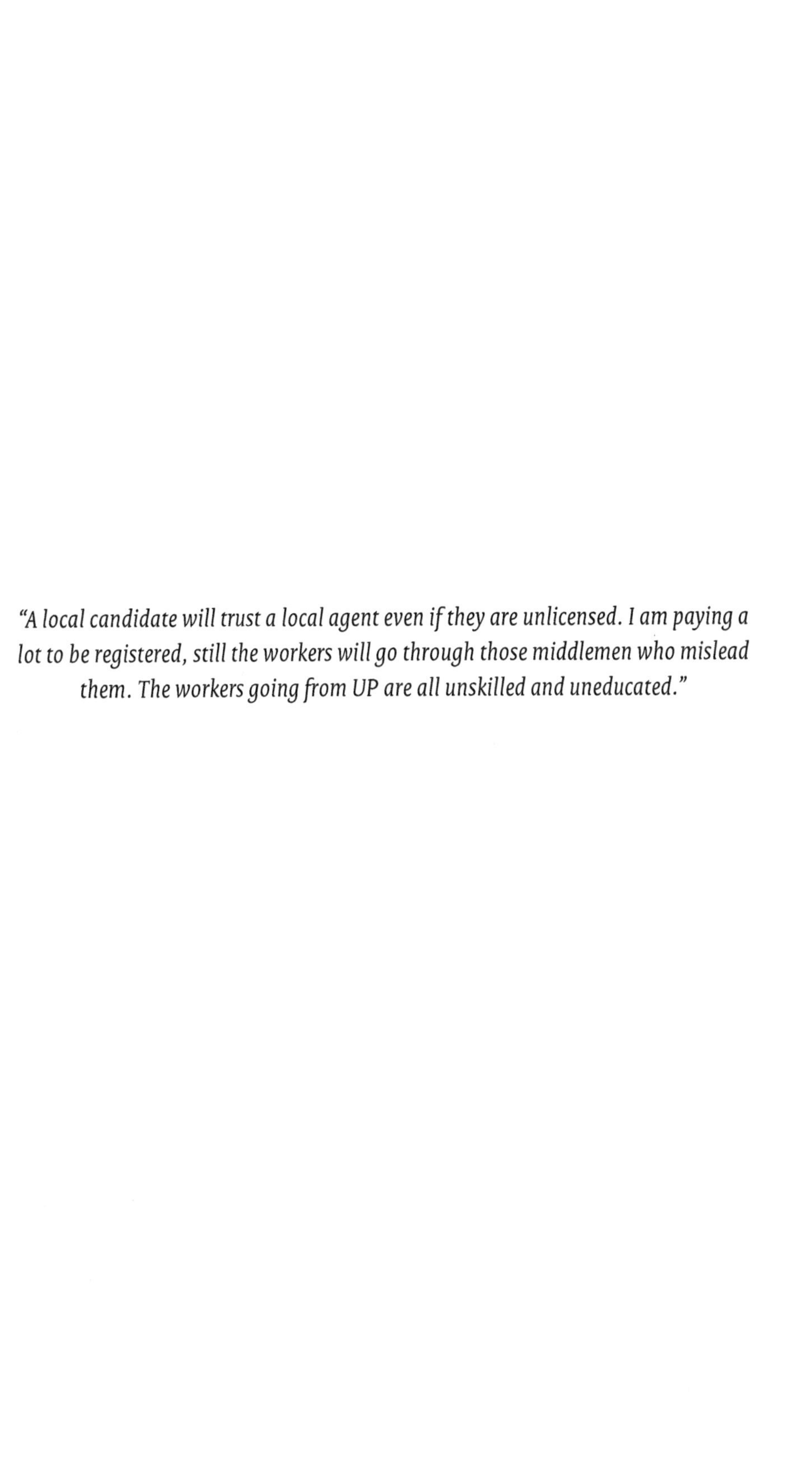

"A local candidate will trust a local agent even if they are unlicensed. I am paying a lot to be registered, still the workers will go through those middlemen who mislead them. The workers going from UP are all unskilled and uneducated."

11

BUILDING TRUST: TWO STEPS FORWARD, ONE STEP BACK

IT ALL BOILS DOWN TO WHOM THEY distrust less. The agents or the government?

You can't walk a yard in the migrant-sending communities without another fraud-agent story popping up. And not one person surveyed migrated legally, grassroots trainers say. "They think we are there to spy on them for the government, to find out if they are receiving money from Saudi. It takes a long time to build that trust."

Alok, Sanjay and Anil Verma go from village to village in several districts of UP, to hold discourses on safe and regular migration, and it has been anything but easy.

"We sat with those in distress, helped them file complaints or claims... only way to reach aspirants. Everyday we have to tweak our modus operandi, improve the information pack... there's so much ignorance on the kinds of visas, the procedures etc.

"They first thought we were either fraud agents or that we were 'Modi-Yogi' people," say the duo who cover Lucknow and Barabanki.

The Indian Prime Minister Narendra Modi and the Chief Minister of UP Yogi Adityanath are viewed with quite a bit of scepticism by much of India's minorities (religious and caste) due to their majoritarian right-wing politics.

"A place like Bareti, for instance, is 70% Muslims. We have to get them to trust us. So we started talking to the pradhans (village heads) and gaining their support and trust."

It's been a slow and uphill task, but one that has provided learning experiences for the trainers as much as for the communities they work in.

"The general feeling we get is that they see no hope here, no chance of getting out of the cycle of poverty. They all have large families with just one or two people working."

The realities of migration are far removed from what printed leaflets can cover.

Anil is with the Voice of Labour organisation and a member of the Bhawan Nirman Karmakar Majdoor Union (BNKMU). While the experiences of the aspirants in his jurisdiction (Sultanpur, Pratapgarh and Amethi) is similar to that of Alok's, the profile of migrants is different.

"There has always been a steady stream of migrants to the Gulf. But since 2008, the numbers have increased. While it used to be predominantly Muslims, now people from the dalit (categorised as lower castes) community go too."

According to him, in 2016 alone, close to 300,000 workers from UP on ECR passports had migrated to the Gulf.

They spend anything between Rs200,000 and Rs350,000 before they leave. That is significantly higher than what we hear is spent in predominantly Muslim communities.

A HARD TO BREAK COLLUSION

In their experience, not a single person went through a registered agent. "When we speak to the registered agents, they say they haven't seen any big demand from aspiring migrants, but unauthorised agents say there are lots of visas. So clearly there is a collusion between the two."

Travel agents also play a role, getting tourist visas, aiding and abetting the irregular migration route.

"They get their visa, contract copy and passport hours before the flight, when there is no time to review or challenge broken promises. They have left their village and are put up in a hotel – on their penny – in a strange city with an international airport. By that point, the decision is irreversible."

It's not that there are no successes, it's just that they are few and far between, where success itself is defined in very narrow and immediate terms.

"They keep sending money home. The worker is not aware that they are spent almost immediately on basic needs and indulgences. They are part of large joint family units, and the money is usually sent to their father or brother, and not to their wife," says Anil.

Because the women, be it Muslim or Hindu, do not go out alone or interact with men outside of their family, even when they do receive money directly they depend on someone else to collect it.

"The workers dream that it has been saved. When they come back, they realise that they have to go back again," he says.

For these workers from India, as in the rest of the world, affordable smartphones have been a lifeline. FB messenger and IMO, he says, play a crucial role in breaking the cycle of isolation and misinformation, even if it comes a tad too late.

The pre-departure trainings that these trainers impart do address all of this. But financial literacy, like all literacy, has to be a continuous learning process.

The BNKMU is trying to garner more support for the forum Pravasi Samik Adhikar that focuses particularly on cross border migrants.

The forum brings together trade unions, NGOs and individuals, and may actually succeed in gaining the trust of these marginalised communities, but it is early days.

E-MIGRATE AND THE CHALLENGES

Vivek Sharma is the Protector of Emigrants for UP. The concerns of the government official reflects that of the trainers.

"UP is the number one state when it comes to ECR passport holders migrating to the Gulf. The second is Bihar."

Both of these states are highly populous, not very well-developed, poor human indices and high social inequalities. Earlier it was Kerala, Tamil Nadu and Punjab.

"When you reach a certain level (of development) you won't go for low-paid, low-skilled jobs. The comparative cost advantage is not in favour of migration," he explains.

"The level of wages in absolute terms is a reason [to migrate] but comparative levels also matter. People in states where the level of wages is not too low compared to what they can earn abroad have a lower propensity to migrate. A small difference between the two [wages] cannot induce [a migrant] to go for the job abroad. The difference between the two wages needs to be significant enough in their view to make them go for a job abroad."

He sees unauthorised agents as the biggest problem to contend with.

"A registered agent goes through a thorough process before they can set up shop and operate. He needs to be a graduate, no criminal records, a Rs50,00,000 bank guarantee, and several other supporting documents."

These high costs do make it difficult for a lot of agents to regularise. A new scheme was introduced where, with a bank guarantee of Rs800,000, you could recruit 100 workers.

There are currently 19 registered agents in UP, and 17 Mumbai and Delhi-based agencies that have branches here.

The PoE doesn't believe in multiple layers of licensing, something countries like Indonesia have tried.

"There's no room for subagents. It will be very difficult to manage. We have had a training for agents and CSOs and are now using mass media to reach remote areas."

Currently, all legal recruitment of ECR passport holders should go through the e-Migrate system, where aspiring workers, employers and agents must all register.

Sharma says there are three main ways in which unauthorised agents function, bypassing the e-Migrate system and other checks and balance that are in place. "They charge the worker and then send him to an agent; or they do an individual application, because they understand the process. Individuals can apply for jobs too, but employer has to be registered on the system, visas and contract attested by embassy in destination."

The third and the 'real fraud', according to him, is sending workers on wrong visas. "Tourist visas... forcing workers to work in captive environment because they are illegal there, too."

He says the agents complain the market is down. Maybe because of recession and also because the system has been tightened. Agents also complain about skill-specific minimum wages, saying it makes our workers less competitive.

"We are not commodities to be price-competitive," he says.

"They get their visa, contract copy and passport hours before the flight, when there is no time to review or challenge broken promises. They have left their village and are put up in a hotel – on their penny – in a strange city with an international airport. By that point, the decision is irreversible."

*"They read out the contract to me.
And I put my thumb impression.
I was 20..."*

SRI LANKA

Published February 2017

POPULATION	21,444,000
NUMBER OF MIGRANTS IN THE GCC	726,331
MAIN RECEIVING COUNTRY GLOBAL	Saudi Arabia
MAIN RECEIVING COUNTRY GCC	Saudi Arabia
REMITTANCES (USD MILLIONS)	6,670
REMITTANCES PERCENTAGE OF GDP	7.9%

Women below 50 years of age must have permission from their families to migrate through regular channels; women with children under five years of age are not allowed to migrate.

12

IN SRI LANKA, MEN ARE FREE, WOMEN HAVE A PRICE TAG

THERE IS A DROUGHT, AND THE PADDY fields don't look promising in Ganewatta. Dotting the square plots are homes in different stages of completion. There are very few clay houses. Here a plot with foundation laid, here a house with stark walls and little else, there another nearing completion.

These houses are a visual representation of the cycle of migration – hopes and dreams, some realised and some interrupted, many in progress.

Kurunegala is one of the largest migrant-sending districts in Sri Lanka. There are 30 divisions in the district and the highest number of migrants go from Kurunegala town, Ganewatta, and Ridigama.

In the market street in Kurunegala town, there are over two dozen manpower companies. There are 100 in the entire district.

Hidden inside new and rundown buildings are plush offices. Up two steep flights of stairs is one such office, with a smartly dressed young women handling the front office. Closed circuit cameras gleam from high up on the wall. The ladies entertain a few questions (yes, we can supply men free of charge; no, there are no Tamil speaking women; no, there is a charge), before the intercom rings. The rest of the conversation moves indoors, to the manager's cabin, which is even plusher. On his desk are a stack of papers and passports. A computer monitor shows a split screen of the camera streaming.

Despite the manager's lack of English, he makes it clear he is suspicious of the exchange.

"Come with a job order. We will talk," he summarily dismisses all interest in ethical recruitment. He hastily adds, probably worried about losing any potential business, "Sri Lankan men you don't pay anything. Women you pay 3,000 dollars."

That's the refrain you hear over and over again. 'Men free, women you pay.' What it translates to is men who wish to migrate pay huge fees throughout the recruitment cycle. So the employer pays nothing or pays a nominal amount.

The demand for female migrants is high, their interest to migrate is dwindling, and the government is making it more difficult for those still interested to go abroad. So women have to be lured with a booking fee of sorts, which is not recognised by the Government. The employer pays all the costs and a premium to hire a female domestic worker.

Ranjith Sisirakumara of the Centre for Human Rights and Community Development notes that there has been a decrease in the number of women migrating. "By 13%. More men are going. Maybe due to new policy and also due to the stories of abuse that are reported. The maid who came with nails in her body is also from this district."

Now agents are paying incentives. "Up to LKR320,000. It is banned by the Foreign Employment Bureau. The principles (employers) have to allocate a minimum of LKR800,000 to get a worker."

A PATRIARCHAL CHECKPOINT

Two years ago, the Family Background Requirement (FBR) was introduced by the Lankan government. Women with children under the age of five require consent from their husband or family. Dilshani feels this only creates room for corruption, as people can get around it.

"These women need the Grama Sevaka Niladari (a village level official) to sign off. It also applies to mothers of children with disability and plantation workers. However, there is little provided in terms of alternative employment for women in the villages itself. Furthermore, when women are paid in advance, their decisions are not taken objectively. Their family spends it. And they are trapped. They have to work contract period or pay back."

Her colleague Titus Wimalasri has mixed feelings about the FBR. "Separation of mothers and children is cruel. I was a teacher before this. I've seen the plight of children of migrant women. We can't deny that."

The FBR first issued in 2013 says mothers with children under five cannot migrate for employment. That they have to submit FBR. A ministry circular in 2015 says all women migrant workers should submit FBR regardless of status. All women, skilled, and unskilled. The FBR is not required for those aged 50 and above, or who have worked abroad earlier, unless the woman has a child with some disability.

"But, we have come across a group of men in Magul Pokuna, not far from Colombo, who force women and their families to migrate against their wishes. From pocketing the signing fee onwards, they get freedom and money, with which they drink and philander. Children are neglected."

These measures seem to be a band-aid treatment for a deep-rooted problem.

"The government is the main benefactor of migration. As we have seen, even after 10 to 15 years, the migrants are unable to meet their goal. But the government continues to receive remittances. It is the government's responsibility to ensure the children are safe and well looked after."

Remittances reach US$7.5 billion a year, comprising 65% of foreign reserves.

Dilshani says that the Foreign Employment Bureau (FEB) has 10 officers for Saudi alone. Yet, it's very difficult to get a response from officials in Saudi.

Sujeewa Lal Dasanayake, chairperson of Lawyers Beyond Borders, Sri Lanka chapter, says there has been a slight decline in departures from 2014 to 2015 (the most recently available statistics).

"In 2015 migrant departures were 263,307; in 2014 it was 300,703. That's a decline of 12.4%."

He feels this decline could be because of a combination of factors – the economic slump in the Gulf, widespread reports of abuses, and also because of the FBR.

"Female departures were 90,677 in 2015 as against 110,486 in 2014, which is a 17.9% decline. In contrast, male migration declined only by 9.2% decline." That's 190,217 (2014) and 172,630 (2015). Departures to the Middle East decreased by 13.5%.

"Approximately 57% of them were in the unskilled workers and housemaid categories. Only 2.4% were under professional categories. About 31.2% were in skilled category."

Sujeewa points out that 64.3% of the 242,431 who migrated in 2015 were male. That's a significant change in the male:female ratio, as previously more women migrated.

SAUDI AND QATAR CONTINUE TO BE THE MOST ATTRACTIVE DESTINATIONS FOR MIGRANTS, REGARDLESS OF GENDER.

2014: 80,480 to KSA; 84,622 to Qatar; 43,552 to Kuwait; and 50,347 to the UAE.
2015: 74,910 to KSA; 65,111 to Qatar; 38,451 to Kuwait; and 43,601 to the UAE.

Despite the overall decline of both migration and the use of agencies, the Lankan Foreign Employment Bureau(FEB) issued 116 new recruitment agency licenses and renewed another 997.

Intriguingly, those seeking to migrate using services of agencies has declined in the same year, from 59% to 44.4%.

"Migrant workers are using other channels, obviously. It's a big challenge to the government if workers use other channels. And the main reason to do so is to subvert current restrictions like the FBR," Sujeewa says.

*"Sri Lankan men you don't pay anything.
Women you pay 3,000 dollars."*

13

DREAMS... PERPETUALLY IN PROGRESS

NAALIKA TARANGANI'S HOUSE IS A MONUMENT TO all that the Gulf stands for in Asian households.

Cans of Tang, empty brown cartons, a blue Nivea tin, dolls in polywrap and teddy bears with tags. The tiny room is crammed with souvenirs her savings could buy, and mark her out as one with a successful stint abroad.

For 15 of the last 24 years, she has lived in two different countries over four different contracts. She first went to Kuwait in 1993, followed by two tours in Dubai, and then spent another five years in Kuwait before coming back home to Sri Lanka. She is not yet sure if this is it for her.

"I was just 19 years old the first time I went. There were 24 members in the family I worked for; in a four-storey house. I was the only maid. But I had no choice but to continue, as I needed the money."

How she was treated and what she endured changed little over the decade. There was a nominal rise in her salary, but most important, she learnt to speak up – to demand at least some of her own terms of employment.

"The children, six and nine years old, were very badly behaved. They would hit me."

Rather telling that the situation for domestic workers has remained stagnant to a large degree, even in a country that had recently passed legislation specific to these workers.

"Though paid on time, I was never allowed out. For the last five years I was with the same employer, never allowed to come back. Even if I went outside the gate to throw garbage, they will watch me. I was not allowed to talk to others. Initially, there was no proper meals. But I put my foot down. Told them clearly that I can't work that way. They allowed me to prepare my own food. Because I threatened to complain to agent. I was paid 60KD first, then it increased to 75KD."

She never got a day off, working till 3 a.m. and up again by 6 a.m. "There were six people initially, then the married daughters came back with their families, so there was more work."

Dilshani Nugawela, whom we spoke to earlier, says the majority of complaints received were from female migrants and more than half from those working in Saudi. As she mentioned earlier, there are 10 Foreign Employment Bureau officers covering Saudi alone, while other destination countries have just one each. The Gulf's largest country continues to be the biggest challenge, with a flood of regular cases and few avenues for resolution.

She shares some figures on the complaints received. In May, 535. 514 in June. 619 in July. 805 in August. 608 in September. And 623 in October.

"These complaints were of regular migrants alone, as only those registered with the bureau can file a complaint. Evidence shows at least 170 irregular migrants attempted to file a complaint," she says.

Most complaints are about salary non-payment, a family's loss of contact with a relative abroad, and harassment. Death continues to be the most common complaint from families of male migrants.

"This is because men go to do construction work, with little training and [are] ill-equipped for the job," she explains.

At the end of the pre-departure training, there is a family day, when the bureau gives information to family members of migrants. Often it's the husband who attends these sessions. But migration puts pressure on family relationships. So they are not there to follow through, she says.

THE 'GOOD' PEOPLE

D M Chandrawathie has never been married. She was the sole caregiver for her orphaned nieces and nephews.

She has returned only recently, and not out of choice. Her body is in a brace, and she squirms in pain as she attempts to lower herself onto the chair.

"I went to Kuwait in 2010, and came back every year. It was a very caring family.

Last month I came back for good. I slipped in the bathroom and fell. For 12 days I was hospitalised. Dislocated my hips. They took very good care of me," she tears up.

Chandrawathie misses her Kuwaiti employers. She was earning 80 KD a month, and had saved enough to construct a house, but has little in the way of savings.

"They were very good to me. They gave me money before I came back and told me when I get better I should come back to them. There were seven children, and the parents. Other workers came and went, I was the one who stayed there throughout."

She had no off day, but that doesn't seem abnormal to her. "Fridays I didn't have much work. Saturdays they took me out. I could prepare my own meals. There were no restrictions. If I can walk properly, I will go back."

Rajeshwari Subramanian is a volunteer educator. She speaks of the pattern. "What we understand is that families of men who have migrated show progress. Not so much in households where women have migrated. Because there is no financial plan for remittances. When a man migrates, the women plan better. They save, invest, build homes. You don't see this with the husbands of women who migrate. They quite often live off the remittances without any thoughts for savings."

Rajeshwari herself is a returnee migrant. She went to Abu Dhabi in 2000, when she was just 26. She went through a seven-day pre-departure training that didn't really help. "The baba had two wives and four children. One child was disabled. So I had to carry her all the time. My wrists were affected badly, and they had to operate on me. They did take good care of me then. Got the neighbour's maid to help out. I was paid 500AED.

"I worked for two years and laid the foundation for my house. That was all I could do. I had a clay house that was washed away."

She went back to Kuwait next, in 2003, for what she describes as a 'horrible' experience. "They didn't give me food even. They had two kids. Wife was at home. There was an Indian driver who cooked. I took care of all the household work. They wouldn't even give me 10 minutes to eat. They will start calling me to come back to work. I would give some change to the driver and ask him to get me some kuboos. I was paid 40 dinars.

"The children, six and nine years old, were very badly behaved. They would hit me. Go to my room and wreck things. Throw my clothes out. I was not allowed to lock my room even. The madam's siblings would ask her why I was not being fed properly."

THE EDUCATORS

Rajeshwari was scared to leave the house because she had heard that the agency or embassy would hit maids who ran away.

In her current work, she understands well why women make ill-informed decisions and stick to it. She also understands why they keep going back abroad. She works in the Rambadagalla area of the Kurunegala district. As we noted earlier in the series, Kurunegala has one of the highest rates of migration in Sri Lanka.

"Almost all the women migrate as housemaids, men go as drivers, etc. We survey and understand the problems they face. There are three categories that we tackle. Families of current migrants, returnees and potential. The returnees are also eager to go back. They have not met the goals they hoped for. Only about 5% seem to have met their goals."

Rajeshwari went back to Saudi after her marriage, along with her husband Veerangan, this time to build her own home. "We went as a couple to work in a household. When we landed in the airport, we were separated. We were kept in separate rooms in the airport. We only received a bun to eat. I didn't know where my husband was. We were taken to another holding room. There were people there who were 'unclaimed' for even a year or two. Our 'owner' sent for my husband and me. They gave us a room together. He was a driver, I was doing household work. The couple had four children. We were there for two years."

Rajeshwari had to return after an accident, and has since had a child who is now seven. "Now we need to secure her future. My husband has gone to Qatar, he is on a second contract now."

She first heard of the educator programme from her niece, and felt she had a responsibility to be part of the process. "To make sure the women who migrate are safe. It is only because of migration that we have been able to buy land and build houses. Whatever the strife, people will go as there is so little opportunity locally."

Rajeshwari does support the FBR policy that disallows women with children under the age of five to migrate. There is a lot of abuse, and the mother has to be around, she stresses.

P G Leelawathie is a colleague of Rajeshwari's. She worked in an insurance firm before doing two stints in Saudi Arabia.

"No awareness. No training. I just gave my passport to an agent and went to Dammam in 2004. The sum total of my Arabic knowledge was 'Salam Aleikum'. I knew only Sinhala, so communication was a big problem. For quite a while I used body language to communicate till I managed to learn some Arabic with help of the children of the house."

Most female migrants are not allowed to keep a mobile and even calls from landlines were restricted, she says.

That experience and the fact that agents were reluctant to talk about workers' rights made her realise that there was a critical need to educate prospective migrants.

Kurunegala echoes such stories. Women exported with little else but a passport and hope for savings.

WORSE THAN MOST

W.P. Nilu stands rocking her toddler son in a makeshift cradle strung from the ceiling as she recounts her days abroad. She lives in abject poverty, in a one-room house furnished with two plastic chairs and a coir floor mat. She picks up her son and straddles him on her hip, introducing him as Dhanush, named after a famous Tamil movie actor from India.

She is hesitant at the start. Completely illiterate and fluent only in spoken Tamil and Sinhala, Nilu borrowed 20,000 Lankan rupees for a passport and medical test, and went to Kuwait in 2007.

Her aged mother, slightly inebriated, had a running commentary on everything her daughter said. The father sat by the door, grinning toothlessly, even as his wife blamed his 'madness' for her daughter being forced to migrate for money.

So why would someone with no reading or writing skills decide to travel thousands of miles overseas?

"The agent encouraged me to," she shrugs. "They read out the contract to me. And I put my thumb impression. I was 20, what options did I have?"

There were 12 members in the Kuwaiti family, including eight kids. "There were two of us maids. Within three months I learnt Arabic."

She earned only 40KD (about US$130) a month and saved nothing. "Had to send money to my older brother, for him to buy a three-wheeler. Which meant I couldn't save anything for myself. I also came back before end of contract, and went back in 2008. They paid me only for four or five months. After that, they were not paying me. So I couldn't fight. I had to cut my losses and come back."

Unlike many other 'serial' migrants, Nilu has not been able to improve the choices she makes. Not just because she was illiterate (Sri Lanka has a high 92% literacy rate), and hence had little access to migration literature nor the ability to review her contract; she also hails from a highly marginalised community – a lower-caste Tamil in the Sinhalese-stronghold of Kurunegala.

Her last foray was to Saudi in 2011 was probably the worst, though she hopes it won't be her last. "I worked in an Egyptian household in Dammam, for only three months. The employer was not good. They were not giving me food properly. Then once a month would take me to their mother's home in Riyadh to work as well. I had to work in all their relatives home. Kids used to be very badly behaved.

"When I refused to work, they beat me up and refused to take me to the agency as I requested. They took me to the police. The police sided with me and asked them to pay me three months' unpaid wages and send me back within 10 days."

Now with a child and no husband/father in sight, and parents incapable of caring for her son, Nilu would find it difficult to bypass the FBR, and will resort to irregular means of migration. With no bankable skills for employment in Sri Lanka, escape from poverty seems highly unlikely. Even as she shares that concern, she flashes a smile tinged with hope.

WHAT IS HOME?

Titus Wimalasri of Caritas says if you ask them why they want to go abroad, the usual answer is 'no house, no land'. But even after 10 to 15 years of working abroad their answer would be the same. "Quite clearly financial planning is not a strong suit."

He also feels that returning migrants, especially those who have lived abroad for many years, sometimes are not accepted back by the family. "And just as often, she may not like living with them. Her world view has changed, and she finds it difficult to adjust to life back in Sri Lanka."

Naalika's story is a case in point. She first helped her parents construct their home, and now is in the process of building her own.

We sit in an incomplete two-room structure – only brickwork, no plaster or paint yet. "My husband is a laborer, so my earnings are important. To finish this house." That's a common tale. After years of migration, few women seem to secure their future. There is always someone else's debts, someone else's dreams to take care of. Parents, husbands, children... and then it seems too late to try and reintegrate into what was once their home.

*"I can't go back. I will have no value in Uganda if I go back like this.
And I need money to pay back debts. I just need to find another job."*

UGANDA

Published July 2017

POPULATION	36,600,000
NUMBER OF MIGRANTS IN THE GCC	80,000
MAIN RECEIVING COUNTRY GLOBAL	Kenya
MAIN RECEIVING COUNTRY GCC	Saudi Arabia
REMITTANCES (USD MILLIONS)	1,182
REMITTANCES PERCENTAGE OF GDP	4.3%

The government placed a complete ban in 2016 on Ugandans' travel abroad for domestic work but has recently signed signed agreements with a number of countries in the Gulf and wider Middle East.

14

IN UGANDA, EVERYONE WANTS TO...
WHAT? ... GO ABROAD

IN THE CENTRE OF KAMPALA, BETWEEN A church, a mosque, and busy shopping complexes, is a large parking lot. Magic Parking is more than a parking lot, though. There are grimy tables and chairs scattered between parked cars, moved every now and then to accommodate a new vehicle. Suds from soapy water float off windshields and land on shoulders and heads of patrons, who barely take the time to brush it off.

A fine layer of red dust settles back on the wet surface, leaving streaks.

Old women bussing tables walk around disinterested in the tales of the young; younger women take orders and serve hot coffee and cold drinks. Somewhere in the background, the latest political news is blaring from a television. Everyone agrees there's not much of a future for youngsters in the country.

"Just take me to Dubai. Leave me in the middle of the road. I will succeed," Murshid Garwango says, or rather, raps.

Latifa Mahmoud, sitting next to Murshid, shakes her head in amusement. She knows success can't be guaranteed. She went to Ras Al Khaimah in November 2014, with the help of a 'friend'. She was promised a job in sales.

"I sold my laptop for 1 million shillings (roughly AED2000 at that point) to pay for visa and tickets to the 'friend'. I landed there and was taken to Lewa Manpower Agency. An Emirati family came and picked me up from the agency. I was taken to a big house in Ras Al Khaimah. Five rooms and three bathrooms downstairs and the same upstairs. There were eight kids and the parents. "I worked 5.30 a.m. to midnight, daily. And when they went camping, I worked 6 a.m. to 1 a.m."

Latifa worked three months before she complained. "They said I had to pay AED10000 (USD2720) to go back. I didn't have that money. I signed a contract for AED1200 at the agency, but was paid only 800."

The hard physical labour without proper food or rest took a toll. "I developed chest pain, back pain. And stomach ulcers because I was never given proper food. They didn't take me to the hospital, even when I offered to pay for medical expenses."

Unable to bear the physical pain, Latifa went to the agency to seek help. "They started screaming at me for coming alone. Saying I should come only with the employer and that I will be accused of stealing money. Then finally they took me to the police station. And they also said I can pay and leave. Where was the money? I told the police that even when I gave money for medicines they didn't get it for me."

The police ordered the employers to take Latifa to the hospital but did little else to alleviate her problem.

Over Ramadan of 2015, Latifa's health deteriorated further. She was not allowed to go out, and her workload increased. Two of the older children, aged 25 and 23, tried intervening.

"They told their parents that it was not fair to make me work alone in such a big house. That I needed help. That was the only kindness, but nothing changed."

It was then that she contacted Yasin Kakande, who was working in UAE as a journalist, and a Migrant-Rights.org contributor.

Yasin spoke to the employers, raising the issue of human rights abuse. The employer denied any wrongdoing. However, they did promise Latifa that she would be sent back after Ramadan, provided no one called to complain.

"Ramadan is a very bad month because there's a lot of work, and we [maids] sleep only for two to three hours.

But even after Ramadan, they did not send me back." When there was no sign of relief, Latifa stopped eating in protest. "I had to protest. Yasin had to speak to them again, then they agreed. I had to pay for my own ticket."

"Just take me to Dubai. Leave me in the middle of the road. I will succeed."

That 'friend' who helped Latifa with her visa? "I never met him. He sent visa and that's all."

Finally, in 2016, Latifa left UAE, with no money and a plethora of health issues that still plague her. During this difficult employment stint, she met Saidiyat, sister of Murshid Garwango.

"My sister went to Tanzania where she met a Ugandan uncle there who helped her go to UAE. He wanted me to go, but we decided my sister would go so I can finish my education."

'Uncle,' like 'friend,' are terms used loosely to describe fellow countrymen. They were promised that she would be working in the home of a family known to uncle. They managed to rustle up $800 and Saidiyat left in Dec 2014.

Garwango has a particular Ugandan inflexion. The almost musical tones interjected with a 'what' – which serves both as a pause and as a check-in on the conversation. When he says, "the first week she said it was all ok. Then things kept getting... what? ... worse", as if in a chorus, everyone at the table echoed his last word.

Latifa met Saidiyat when she went out of the house to dispose of garbage. "I used to bring her some money. But her situation is bad."

She has a phone hidden away, and communication is sporadic. "My sister is very very sick, she has been beaten. Every time we speak to her she cries. She complains."

Uncle is no longer helpful, says Garwango.

The happy, successful anecdotes are mere myths that each new emigrant hopes to experience for real. At the moment, the stories that come out are all dire.

Yet, Murshid Garwango is certain his journey will be different, even if his landing were to be bumpy. "Just take me to Dubai. Leave me in the middle of the road... what?... I will succeed," he repeats

Dusk falls and we sit there sipping teas. What if they didn't go to the Gulf, and worked here?

"The politicians are too corrupt."

"There are no employment opportunities."

"It's better to go to a foreign country."

A few days later, in a different setting, in a bar inside a church complex, an elite club of intellectuals gather for their monthly meeting. There are lawyers and consultants, engineers and journalists, sipping their tonic water, their chatter segueing between world affairs and local politics.

We discuss the spate of reports on the abuse of Ugandan workers, men and women, in the Gulf. The educated gentlemen think it's the media exaggerating again – after all, the Gulf is where dreams come true.

"It's good for Ugandans to go abroad and work," they all say. Then the familiar refrain.

"There's so much corruption." "Inflation and salaries don't keep up."

"No wonder our young want to go abroad to secure their future." Uganda struggles with an 80% unemployment and underemployment rate.

THE BREADWINNERS AND THEIR PATRIARCHS

A couple of days after the Magic Parking meeting, we hit the road to Luweero, about 60 km from Kampala. The roads are caked with red soil and lined with fertile agricultural fields. Every surface has a coat of burnt orange dust; even the cattle reflect the colour. With a large loaf of bread and a bag of sugar, we are ready to visit Mohamed Lukwago, a village elder. We pick up his daughter ZamZam Lukwago from the novelty store she runs in the town square, a 15-minute drive away from her home.

She returned after a three-year stint in Kuwait, and with the money saved, opened this little store and bought a plot of land to build her own house. To actually build a house, ZamZam – who has a one-year-old daughter and is separated from her husband – has to go abroad again.

Right before we reach our destination, we run into Abdul Wahab Kityo, who is herding his cows back to the cattle shed adjoining his home. "He has a lot of experience," ZamZam grins.

Kityo has 17 children. One wife is in Cairo and one of his daughters, Joweriya Nakawoya, works in Dubai. She went to Dubai with a family 'friend' who had come to Uganda on a holiday.

"We paid about 1 million shilling as commission to the friend. They said she would be paid USD200 but she sent back only $100 twice. They don't allow her to have a phone, and she talks from the employer's phone. She complained about the food. They give her the baby's leftovers," Kityo deadpans in dialect.

The family friend is no longer of help. And Joweriya herself doesn't want to come back. "We are still paying off the debts, and she wants to save. She still has hopes."

A group of children return home from school. Batiga Tahiah changes out of her school uniform and sidles up to her father. He is keen on sending Batiga abroad. She is 20 but looks years younger. "Going there is better than going to school," he says, and she eagerly nods her agreement.

She does enjoy school and history is her favourite subject. She speaks softly, almost in whispers. "I have a passport. I am willing to go to help my family. Build a nice house."

Kityo is not aware of the ban on Ugandan women travelling to the Gulf. "I only know Saudi Arabia is not safe. So will not send my daughters there. Other places are ok. The problem is finding a correct agent, to trust someone. Even those who are educated don't get professional jobs, they still go as housemaids."

He looks expectantly. "Would you be able to find her a job?"

ZamZam takes leave quickly; it's raining, and we still have to meet her family before heading back to Kampala for the night.

"Complaining is no use. She gets paid $200 every month. So she will finish her contract and come back in August."

BRICK BY BRICK

As the car drives into the front yard, you can see the remains of a disused room in the foreground, and a larger, newer concrete structure in the middle of the plot of land.

The before and after exhibits. Three of Mohamed's daughters have worked in the Gulf, and the family owes their affluence to them. The front room has large sofas and dozens of coir mattresses rolled up in one corner of the room adjacent to it. There's a kitchen and wash facilities somewhere beyond these rooms.

On one wall is a large fading poster of Moammar Gadaffi, who is something of an African hero.

The patriarch is seated on the sofa, his wife on a cushion by his feet. The daughter and grandchildren are busy with chores.

He has several children; "We don't count, we have as many as Allah destines." Later the interlocutor says there may be children from other wives or mistresses, and it was a sensitive matter.

So the discussion revolves around three daughters: Sophia, who works in Saudi Arabia, Madina in Dubai and ZamZam who has returned from Kuwait.

Sophia went abroad in 2013 and hasn't saved much as she has to pay for her children's education.

Zamzam's is the success story. A trained nurse, she went to Kuwait in 2012 to take care of a premature baby. She worked for three years, providing round-the-clock care for the child, and came back well remunerated.

"I am still in touch with the family, they were very good to me. I could save a lot."

In February 2016, Madina travelled to Dubai. They paid an agent 1.7 million shillings, which they have already recovered with her earnings. Now she saves, the father says with pride.

The mother, who sat in silence until then, joins the conversation. "We see the news [of workers' abuse], and we are worried. Madina calls every Friday. She is not mistreated, but there's lots of work. Complaining is no use. She gets paid USD$200, every month. So she will finish her contract and come back in August."

Zamzam would have been no more than 18 or 19 when she first went to Kuwait. What drove her to make that move?

"The decision was made by the family, and if an opportunity came, the girls would go. As Muslims, we know God destined (rizik)," Mohammed, the retired driver, says.

As one other migrant told us, for many Ugandans the Arab is as good as Islam itself, so going to Saudi Arabia is seen as a privilege.

His wife extends an overflowing basket of mangoes as a gift, and suddenly the bread and sugar seem a sorry offering.

As we leave their home, the father calls out from his seat, "If there is ever an opportunity, a good safe one, tell us. For our daughters."

The story is eerily similar across continents and cultures. In impoverished families, a woman willing to migrate is seen as a ticket out of poverty. From villages in Indonesia and Sri Lanka, Nepal and Bangladesh, Uganda and Cameroon, women both young and old make risky journeys with little orientation, to help achieve dreams of the fathers and sons, brothers and husbands. As was the case with Saidiyat, Zamzam, Joweriya and in months to come, Batiga.

"I developed chest pain, back pain. And stomach ulcers because I was never given proper food. They didn't take me to the hospital, even when I offered to pay for medical expenses."

15

IN THE LAND OF FRIENDS AND UNCLES, EVERYONE IS AN AGENT

AS ONE LANDS IN ENTEBBE, THE MAGNIFICENT Lake Victoria sparkles, almost colourless against the relief of the rich greenery and deep red soil. The Ugandan passengers on the flight all crane to catch a glimpse of their home, before their feet touch the ground. There's an eagerness you see time and again, on flights 'home' – to Kathmandu or Colombo, Kochi or Dacca. The returning sons and daughters of the soil feasting with their eyes, from up in the sky, upon what they've missed for years. It's a searing contrast to take off from the monotony of brown in the Gulf and land in something so verdant.

Some of those coming back are the ones who will help others go abroad – they have job offers and 'free visas' in their kitty, and for a not-so-small fee (1 million to 2 million shillings), become stealthy recruitment agents.

In Uganda, migration of lower-skilled workers (outside of Africa) is a rather recent trend. Governments, communities, NGOs and recruitment agencies are learning trial by error; unfortunately, those errors cost workers their lives and livelihoods. The lexicon of migration used by stakeholders is itself a problem – 'export maids', 'license to export labour' – a commodification from the start.

Atuko Grace, Principal Labour Officer of the Ministry of Gender, Labour and Social Development, does not deny the lack of preparedness.

"In 2013, we signed a bilateral agreement with Saudi Arabia, and we had challenges," she says, referring to the large number of abuse cases reported. "Girls were being taken without pre-departure training. The Government was involved in the training of security guards etc, but not for domestic workers."

NO EXPERIENCE, NO TRAINING

When cases of abuse were widely reported, Uganda banned its female citizens from going to the Gulf as domestic workers. In May, a Parliamentary decision was taken to lift the ban, allowing workers to be deployed only to countries with which Uganda has signed an agreement.

"We recently signed an agreement with Jordan. And we have revisited the Saudi agreement. We don't want to make the same mistake we did while signing the agreement with Saudi. So we have called for proposals to establish for pre-departure training centres."

Earlier, when domestic workers were being sent through formal channels, the pre-departure training was done by agencies themselves.

"About the language, the culture, how to behave in the household, how to use electronic appliance etc. But it's not a module. It's what the agency decided was important."

While agencies are licensed by the Ministry's Externalisation department, the pre-departure training itself was not supervised or informed by the Government.

As rudimentary as the training was, when the ban came into effect, it stopped. The recruitment agents we spoke to say none of them serviced domestic workers job orders now.

Unsurprisingly, the ban has been ineffective, and workers continued to go abroad. When you have uncles and friends, what need for agents?

The Ministry doesn't have numbers, but Atuko says they receive a lot of complaints from families of victims. "Usually they would have gone through Kenya or Tanzania to the Gulf countries. Then the families tell us they are stuck there without a visa, or in a bad situation."

SUCCESS AT WHAT COST?

"Most of them (migrants) have left illegally. They have heard from a friend or relative. The cooperate with those people, complicit in those lies till they leave and land in trouble," says Grace Mukwaya, the Executive Director of Platform for Labour Action (PLA), an NGO that provides legal aid and educates workers, both those in the local labour market and those who migrate.

Uganda's minimum wage has remained at 6,000 shillings (less than USD$2), unchanged since it was set in 1984.

"No one gets paid that little, but because it's so low one can't negotiate fairly. Then people started hearing about opportunities. The bilateral agreement with Saudi in particular, even when halted, gave new aspirations to Ugandans," she says.

"Many people suffer, many people benefit. Those who succeed, their lives are changed. The success stories encourage more people."

Mukwaya's cousin is in Abu Dhabi, too. "He was getting 2,000 shillings a day here. He went there and now earns 1 million shillings. He says 'I work very hard, am paid very little. I will look for another job.' But he never says he will come back," she points out.

Osman and his friend recently moved to Abu Dhabi and reached out to Migrant-Rights.org. What he was promised was AED2000 as a security guard, and what he received was AED500, working in a bakery. Despite conflict with the employer and being stranded in the city, he doesn't want to leave.

"I can't go back. I will have no value in Uganda if I go back like this. And I need money to pay back debts. I just need to find another job."

Osman and Mukwaya's cousin, like thousands of migrants to the Gulf before them, will suppress the hardship and play up the successes when they finally go back home. Until then, they do everything in their capacity to make good of a terrible situation.

In general, and more so since the ban, many Ugandans go to the Middle East as domestic workers through places of worship, both churches and mosques.

"A Ugandan worker in the Middle East might get a deal to bring in domestic workers. I've heard they get as high as USD$300 per worker. They often reach out through the pastors, imams, preachers and local leaders, each getting a cut, and who in turn encourage the women to take these jobs without any awareness of the consequences," Mukwaya complains.

The usual spiel goes something like this: "God has done something wonderful for my aunty, He is going to take you to..." After a year on the streets of Kampala without a job, this would be an easy sell.

TRAFFICKER VS AGENT

Trafficking is rife. And the word is also used as a shield to deflect attention.

Nooh Mayambala runs a recruitment agency (mainly providing security guards to the UAE) and is not pleased that all the ills of labour export are blamed on recruitment agents.

He is the Secretary General of the Uganda Association of External Recruitment Agencies. Weeks before the ban is to be lifted, they are holding a workshop in an upmarket Kampala hotel. During a coffee break, we find him and his colleagues are deep in conversation and interrupt.

"We [the agencies] have tried to regulate ourselves; we are working on monitoring the situation, and yes, we are lobbying for the lifting of the ban, after some provisions have been included, of course," he said.

"Officially Uganda had provided domestic workers to Saudi alone. We [the agents] had just started work on it, as we had no previous experience. Then the traffickers stepped in quickly. You can never trace those who have suffered to a licensed agent," he says, defending his kith.

The 'trafficker' is the bogeyman, faceless, nameless and someone else's problem.

So does that mean that all the agencies follow ethical processes, and the workers they deploy face no problems? There's a steely silence, the meeting ends.

It's true that the association has been more proactive than the government itself. They had already made reconnaissance trips to Jordan and met with the recruitment association there.

Mukwaya feels that, although there are definite problems with recruitment agents, at least the workers will know where they are going and what kind of work they are expected to do.

TRICKED AND TRAFFICKED

A PLA study on trafficking looked at confirmed victims of international trafficking (VIT) between 2010 and 2016.

It revealed that most of the VIT respondents were taken to Saudi Arabia (37.2%), followed by Kuwait (18.6%), the United Arab Emirates (9.3%), Oman (7%), Kenya (7%), Qatar (4.7%), China (2.3%) and other countries (14%).

According to the Ugandan Ministry of Internal Affairs Annual report on trafficking, a total of 424 persons were victims of transnational trafficking.

The breakdown is as follows:

Kuwait (98), Syria (83), DRC (72), Malaysia (43), India (35), UAE(15), Turkey(13), Kenya (11), Qatar (10), South Sudan (10), Thailand (08), Saudi Arabia (04), Oman (03), Iraq (03), China (02), South Africa (02), Germany (02), USA (02), Rwanda (02), the Czech Republic (01), Lebanon (01), UK (01), The Netherlands (02) and Switzerland(01).

"Most of the girls are not Muslims but are subjected to wearing hijabs. They are not told this earlier."

FROM IGNORANCE TO STRIFE

"The problem is that the government does not promote the list of registered or licensed recruitment agents. There's a list available in the Ministry but how many people go there to see it? It is important to educate workers about going through right channels. The list should be available in local council offices in the villages," she suggests.

"When we get complaints, most workers are not even aware who took them, where they land," Mukwaya says.

Moses Binoga is the Coordinator of the National Trafficking in Persons Task Force. His is a one-man office within a sprawling complex that houses the Interior Ministry's different departments, including passport issuance. Right at the entrance to the complex is a large poster advising people against trafficking, and across from that signage is a tent where hundreds of citizens are lined up to get their passport paperwork done.

Like most of Uganda, it's a vibrant and communal space; women in crisply starched colourful frocks and men in smart suits buzz around. Strangers become friends in a matter of minutes. They bond over a familiar tribe name, a smile, a common destination...

With that atmosphere in the background, it's somewhat easy to understand why Binoga feels the problems 'housemaids' face in the GCC are both of their own making and that of the employer.

"Our Ugandans are not sensitised to the work there. Even those who go through agencies don't have proper information. Their expectations are not met due to insufficient information. They don't understand the culture or the work requirement." Binoga continues, "Then there's this big problem about food. They are not told they will get only bread. For us, if we don't eat Ugali [maize meal] we feel we haven't eaten. And in our culture eating leftovers is an insult."

He adds, "Most of the girls are not Muslims but are subjected to wearing hijabs. They are not told this earlier." Binoga feels pre-employment briefing for employers is as important as a pre-departure orientation for workers.

"The workers are expected to do everything without enough rest or food. Forced to work even when sick. In fact, many contracts in Saudi state that if the worker doesn't finish the contract then they pay back recruitment fees."

Though irregular recruitment is an offence in itself and promotes trafficking (recruited through deceitful means, debt bondage and exploitation), unless a complaint is filed, it is not considered trafficking.

"Many Arab recruitment agencies operate here illegally using loopholes. There are two kinds of licence available. One internal and one external. They get an internal licence, find workers, and send them abroad by collaborating with criminals," he says.

In the swirling mass of people, under the shade of trafficking posters, one is bound to bump into both would-be victims and trafficking collaborators. Right now though, the air is filled with hope as the chimaera of wealth and success in the Gulf holds strong against reports to the contrary.

Acclimatising to life in the Gulf continues to be a big problem for Ugandans, who are used to a rather vibrant, community-based lifestyle. Proper pre-departure training will align expectations with reality.

"When we get complaints, most workers are not even aware who took them, where they land."

A 19-hour work day, seven days a week, for less than 40 cents an hour.

ETHIOPIA

Published November–December 2017

POPULATION	102,400,000
NUMBER OF MIGRANTS IN THE GCC	460,000
MAIN RECEIVING COUNTRY GLOBAL	United States
MAIN RECEIVING COUNTRY GCC	Saudi Arabia
REMITTANCES (USD MILLIONS)	806
REMITTANCES PERCENTAGE OF GDP	1%

The vast majority of Ethiopian migrant workers to the Middle East are female domesitc workers. Ethiopia banned domestic workers to Saudi and Kuwait in 2014, following mass deportations and recruitment bans from the two Gulf states.

16

THE BAN IS A BLESSING... FOR THE TRAFFICKERS IN ETHIOPIA

ABOUT 170,000 ETHIOPIANS WERE DEPORTED FROM SAUDI Arabia between November 2013 and March 2014. Four years later, Ethiopia is yet to fully reintegrate and rehabilitate these returnees, and now has to grapple with the deportation of another 100,000 workers.

Since the first en masse deportation, neither Ethiopia nor Saudi Arabia has done much to improve the status of this highly marginalised group. The stories only get more desperate.

In 2014, Ethiopia dovetailed Saudi's mass deportation with a ban of its own. Temporary at the time of the announcement, the blanket ban on Ethiopian women migrating for domestic work is still in place. And as bans go, it's a complete failure that only served to make the situation of migrants more precarious.

Every returnee and potential migrant shrugs at the idea of the ban doing any good.

"Ban? The only thing that happens is that the price goes up. Doesn't stop anyone, and the black market becomes profitable," says Fatima Hassan, who has two daughters working in the GCC.

Migrant-Rights.org spoke to potential migrants, returnees, and their families. Most of those we interviewed found a passage to the Gulf during the ban.

The most disheartening truth of the pre- and post-ban era is that little has changed to protect female migrant workers. In Saudi Arabia and the rest of the GCC, new laws and regulations - notwithstanding attitudes towards domestic workers - continue to be indifferent at best and cruel at worst.

There's only the occasional societal outrage on the fringes of gruesome incidents like that of Adesech Sadik or Kasturi.

Sadik was filmed by her employer in Kuwait, as she was pleading for her life, hanging from a seventh-floor balcony. Kasturi's arm was chopped off by her Saudi employer when she attempted to escape the abusive household.

...long-term plans are encompassed in short-term projects, often driven by donor-agendas, susceptible to change alongside donor priorities...

There is no information on what justice has been served by the two countries, and what punishment the employers received (Sadik's employer was arrested, but no updates are available on the status of the case). These are just two of the thousands of cases of abuse that origin country embassies receive in the GCC states. Repatriating the workers is seen as resolution, while the employers and state get away scot-free.

LESSONS NOT LEARNT

For Ethiopia, which has the longest legacy of migration to the Gulf from the Horn of Africa, the experiences have not really served as a learning opportunity. It has grappled with internal conflict, drought and unemployment. With so little opportunity at home, prohibiting its most marginalised citizens from going abroad has only assured a steady stream of business for traffickers and smugglers.

Addis Ababa is the headquarters for the African Union and home for regional offices of the biggest development organisations, UN, and other donor agencies. That means long-term plans are encompassed in short-term projects, often driven by donor agendas, susceptible to change alongside donor priorities, regardless of needs on the ground.

There doesn't seem to be a cohesive plan for the country as a whole, experts we speak to point out.

Citizens have no choice but to look outward. There are three levels of migration, three composite regions that an average low-skilled potential migrant recognises and hopes to land in. Getting out of their village to Addis Ababa; getting out of Ethiopia to other African countries, and getting out of Africa to the Middle

East. Every path out of their home and into these regions is a risky one. Crossing through war zones in Yemen and conflicts in Somaliland at the mercy of traffickers and smugglers, they then land in countries that don't have the laws or will to protect them.

"There are no job opportunities, no technical or financial resources to start their own business, no rehabilitation and reintegration process. So returnees always strive to go back. With the ban, they are now using brokers instead of registered agents. They all want to re-migrate," says Mebratu Gebeyehu, a consultant who works on migration policies.

Like Salam and Saba, who are neighbours and friends, they have both trained as hairdressers and take customers on the mud ledge outside their home in Addis Ketama, an impoverished sub-city in the capital. If their current situation doesn't change, they would like to migrate again.

Saba has worked in Saudi for three years and then a year in Sharjah. She wants to move to Dubai, where she believes her life would be much better.

Salam is not so sure. "If things are smooth here, I will stay back. I worked for nearly three years in Abu Dhabi. I had to come back because of poor health."

Though she was paid her 600 dirhams salary on time, the employer deducted two months salary for costs of recruitment. "They were ok, but weekends, Thursday to Saturday, they would lock up the house and we didn't even have access to kitchen or food. There was a Filipino maid with me. We had to get food from outside."

Saba was not so lucky. "I was there on a four-year contract. The family I worked for in Riyadh were poor themselves. So I wasn't paid regularly. In fact, for the last six months, I was not paid at all. I preferred work in Emirates, at least there you have some freedom."

Saba feels if she and Salam were to set up a salon, they would earn as much as they would in the Gulf. "But not if we work for someone here. That won't pay us much at all."

Their stint abroad has not ensured even the slightest of financial stability for the women.

According to a survey of returnees in 2014, on average, every female or male migrant had 3.8 dependents on remittances. Less than 31% of respondents said their remittance was saved back home.

As Gebeyehu points out, "A girl who works there sends money to her parents or siblings or husband. They assume the family will save money for them. She comes back and realises her assumption was wrong. There's no financial planning."

'EVERYBODY LIVES HIS OWN FATE'

Laila Wasihun knows exactly what that feels like. She takes a long sip of her soda. She has spent the morning walking with us through the streets of Kombolcha where she works as a community mobiliser, listening to people's aspirations and fears, their longing and desperation for a better life. She was more than an empathetic listener.

A returnee and community mobiliser, she says stories of caution are rarely received well.

She was one of them four years ago, on the brink of moving to Taif, Saudi Arabia; she was that girl about whom a parent fretted for three years and four months. Now, at 26, she is this person who tries to gently and firmly steer families away from making ill-informed choices.

"People do ask for advice. And there's also a huge resistance from those who have never been abroad when I offer mine." Dr Daniel Keftasse quotes an oft-repeated saying in Oromo and Amharic. 'Everybody lives his own chance/fate.'

You can line up any amount of evidence against going abroad, but the migrant will take his 'chaara' or 'ool', he says (both terms mean chance in Oromo and Amharic).

"What about the probability of success? No one listens," says Keftasse, who works in the Arsi highlands (about four hours from Addis). His organisation, Harmee Education for Development Association (HEFDA), tries to keep girls in school long enough to either not migrate at all, or migrate with knowledge and skills.

Laila shares her story from taking a fateful chance to now helping others make an educated choice.

"In Taif, I worked for a young couple who had three children. The first year I worked only at their home. Then I was asked to work at madam's mother's house nearby, as her Indonesian maid had left. I would be up by 5.30 a.m. and would not be able to get to bed until well past midnight."

LIVING ON LOW EXPECTATIONS

The expectations of a good work environment are so low, Laila maintains they treated her well, like family. "They even took me with them to Dubai on a holiday.

After the first three months they gave me a phone, bought me air time, I called home every week," she reminisces fondly.

But the workload was too much. She tried negotiating a pay raise and was promised one after four years. "But I could not hang on any longer. I could not take the load. For six months they resisted my plea to go back home. Then they gave in. Sent me back with gifts."

For 800 riyals a month – which was paid on time and regularly, she reminds us gratefully – she worked two homes, short on sleep and rest.

A 19-hour work day, seven days a week, for less than 40 cents an hour.

Laila would have liked to continue working, realising a few dreams of her own. "My first aim was to help my parents, brothers and sister. Now my brother has his own garage… my family is doing well. But I haven't been able to do much for myself."

Laila is also concerned that thousands of her sisters are migrating with inadequate or wrong information, unprepared to face challenges that are likely to arise. Because there's no proper information reaching them, they go for advice from peers that seems easy but is not. "Some encourage workers to run away so they would earn more. They shouldn't. Their whole life can be ruined by an ill-thought decision."

The pressure from parents is far higher than from the girls themselves."

CHIMERA OF SUCCESS

Gebeyehu says that in the past there were some who managed to change their lifestyles because of money from Jeddah. They still serve as an example, even if you don't see that many success stories now.

"For the community, it's a way out of poverty. There's a positive perception to migration, despite the reporting to the contrary. Unless this changes there won't be any participation in law enforcement."

The perception is so deep-rooted that it even creeps into negotiations on arranged marriages. "There's been a practice to send wife or daughter to Jeddah. 'Will you send your daughter to Jeddah?' is what they ask when a marriage is being fixed," says Gebeyehu.

Keftasse reiterates this. "People don't understand how migrants live there. They only recognise that they send money. The pressure from parents is far higher than from the girls themselves. By the time they are 17 or 18 they are groomed to go abroad. The ones who come back are ashamed of any humiliation they might have faced and don't feel comfortable speaking about experiences there. So they lie or hide the truth."

His organisation identified a high correlation between school dropouts and migration when they worked actively on migration between 2013 and 2015. But these projects are short term, as donor's interests change, too.

"The centre of our work is education, to keep them in school, give them hope. To help them see possibilities in the country. We are also challenged when we have educated people who can't find a job. If they do want to migrate, we ask them to go with a skill. But they go to the Arab world only as domestic workers."

Only two or three out of ten girls find a job after school and they feel there's no hope or future in this country, he says.

Migration and more so illegal migration is a big business.

According to Keftasse, "Everyone makes money, governments, brokers... and it's not about remittances alone, it's being relieved from the burden of unemployment for the government."

A FAILED BAN

Information on migration comes from two opposing viewpoints. The government programmes focus on negative aspects of migration. The returnees play it up. A study showed people trust returnees over governments.

"In Jimma, Dessie, Arsi, migration has become a culture, more than an economic move, more than employment. For someone to be considered successful they have to migrate. So much so, boys as young as seven or eight years attempt to migrate, for cattle herding," Keftasse says.

Asfaw Ambaw is an official with the Social and Labour Department, Dessie Town, South Wollo. He knows he could well be fighting a losing battle.

"The trends in migration has been shifting these last ten years, but migration continues, and is in fact on the rise. Earlier they went regularly, through agents. Now they go on tourist visa or Umrah visa. The brokers are now family members themselves, facilitating irregular migration," he says.

Because they are an intricate part of the community, no one is willing to call them out or report them.

Complaints arise only when a worker goes missing.

Keftasse also speaks of the tug-of-war with agents in his project area. Even as they appeal to parents to keep the girls in school till they turn 18, the agents work on the parents to send them abroad. "The government and society are not well prepared to handle this issue of illegal agents."

Right after the ban came into place, licenses were cancelled and agencies were closed. His reading is that those very agents were driven underground, sending workers illegally and profiting more than ever. And that's something migrants and officials both agree on.

17

"I WANT TO ESCAPE"

'WE HAVE NEVER BEEN COLONISED' IS A refrain that echoes in every conversation you have in Ethiopia, from the front office staff at the hotel to the taxi driver, from the community worker to the petty shop trader.

A proud refrain against the backdrop of large-scale Chinese investments and schemes driven by donors from every rich country imaginable, with poverty so extreme, corruption so high, and the middle class a minority.

About 370 km from Addis Ababa, en route to Djibouti, Kombolcha is an emerging industrial town in South Wollo region. The Chinese are building industrial parks, tailoring units, and the most basic of infrastructure in and around the area.

There is an effort to generate employment opportunities through these different projects. But Najat is not buying it. Her heart is set on Dubai.

Her brother is the gatekeeper of their home and her dreams.

The family runs a coffee and refreshments shop from the front room of their home.

"The father makes the decision," a community worker whispers, "So you will meet him first and then the girl who wants to go to the Jeddah."

"I don't even know who will pick me up from the airport, or whose house I will work in."

Jeddah is a generic term used for anywhere in the Gulf region.

A young man of slight build and one too many worry lines around his eyes enters the room. We learn the older woman and young girl who were at the till are his mother and youngest sister.

Aragie Yemer, all of 28, is the 'father', which is a placeholder word for the male head of the family.

He first learnt of the Middle East in 2006, when many youngsters from the village sought their fortunes there.

"I had no plans to go myself. I make do running this tea shop. But now my sister wants to go and change her life. She is 22 and has been wanting to go since 2014. She feels there are more options there. Friends of hers, even younger than her, have been talking about it," he pauses, gathering his thoughts.

He seems displeased with his sister's decision but knows she will wear him down sooner or later. When a person wants to migrate, they will. Regardless of what obstacles line their way. A realisation that still hasn't dawned upon authorities.

"I hold her passport," he continues reluctantly. "I am worried because of the ban. She will go to Saudi if the ban is lifted; if not, will go to Dubai."

The reason Aragie is trying to sway his sister to stay is not just to exert his power. "We hear so many negative stories from those countries. We don't want her to go even if the ban is lifted. She is a Grade Eight dropout, doesn't think she can earn here."

Aragie feels she can get into any number of vocations – petty trading, hairdressing, tailoring.

Hairdressers, petty traders, tailors… you can't walk 500 metres without tripping over one of these 'businesses.' These vocations continue to be the weak foundation on which many policies are built to counter migration.

Imaan, the youngest sister, is listening keenly to the discussion. The 15-year-old has dropped all pretence of helping her mother at the counter.

The decision her brother takes about Najat, the older sister, will impact her life too.

Shy and soft-spoken, Imaan says even her friends in school – Grade Nine– speak of going to the Middle East all the time. They are all convinced their lives would change only then. "I am tempted too."

ANYWHERE BUT HERE

Najat enters even as her brother lists the career options in front of her. She is unmoved. She minces no words. "I don't want to go to Saudi, ban or no ban. I want to go to Dubai."

They are not aware that the ban is for all overseas migration from Ethiopia.

Najat hasn't even been to Addis. "I will go there when I have to fly to Dubai. It doesn't scare me. I haven't convinced my family... yet." Yet... her mother and brother seem resigned to the fact they can no longer stop her. Her sister looks cautiously happy.

"I don't know how much I will earn. Where I will work. I will stay for three years, send money back home... money for me." Her dreams are generic. A business, a better life.

"At this point, I just know my life has to change." Life in the Gulf is her Hail Mary pass to a better life.

"I just trust my father to get all the information. I know I am not going through a regular agent."

So far they have paid only for the passport, but expect to pay another 9,000 to 11,000 Ethiopian birr (USD$330 to $400) for her to be able to travel.

Abeba Sied Adam is also at a similar juncture. In her case, she is being urged to migrate by her father, and as she claims, her seven year-old daughter.

Her passport and medical reports are being processed so she can go to Dubai as a domestic worker. She shrugs when she hears of a ban. Everyone is going to Dubai, she smiles.

Twenty-seven-year-old Abeba works at a nightclub in Komblocha. She is candid about her life and work in Ethiopia, despite her seven year-old lounging on the narrow cot in one corner of the room, listening to her mother speak.

Her paperwork has been with the broker for about three months now. She has paid him 6,000 birrs so far; savings from her work at the nightclub. "I make good money there, about 7,000 birrs (USD$290). And if I can't raise more money I will ask my father for help. I have to go."

Abeba wasn't really planning to migrate. "My father lives in Wuchulu (90kms from Komblocha) and in his village he heard of a broker sending women from the community to the Middle East, and convinced me to meet him."

Her father, she claims, doesn't know she works in a nightclub and earns well.

"I just trust my father to get all the information. I know I am not going through a regular agent."

The lady who took her in when she ran away from her parents home years ago, to work in the club, has warned her to be careful in the Gulf. "She was telling me about people stealing organs." An accusation thrown in so casually, taken so lightly.

Abeba cannot give room for any doubts in her mind, now that the decision to go abroad has been made.

"My daughter will live with her grandparents. She wants me to go. She sees other small kids who receive gifts from their mothers who live abroad. She wants to buy a house also. This is rented," she says, waving her arms dismissively at the blue walls of her one-room home.

Across the doorway, in one corner is a coal-fuelled stove and some utensils. An uncovered window provides the only natural light source for the room. The remnants of a birthday celebration are still up on the wall.

The 'she' who wants a house and small gifts just turned seven the week before. She pulls out a packet of photos from under the pillow and gives it to her mother.

In frills and bows, surrounded by her friends and a doting mum, a rich white cake and gifts, she glows in her birthday photos.

Abeba pulls out a photo of herself in full make-up and *intricate shurubas.* "Use this. I don't look good today... don't take my photo. Take me if you want," she laughs, not quite joking.

There's just that fleeting moment of doubt and insecurity before she goes back to her confident and chirpy self.

"I will stay [in Dubai] forever if I like it. I've been talking to people who have come back from the Gulf. I understand the place. In two months I can learn the language."

Does she plan to speak to the employer before she travels?

She looks nonplussed. "I don't even know who will pick me up from the airport, or whose house I will work in." The uncertainty is still worth the risk for Abeba. "I want to escape."

As we cross the road from her home to the waiting car, a lady from the neighbourhood stops. She has a story too. Someone's missing and she needs help tracking her down in Dubai.

This would happen a handful of times, people lost, people in search of someone... people floundering.

LACK OF OPTIONS

There is a lack of cross-fertilisation between migration and employment policies, says Ruchika Bahl, Chief Technical Adviser, Project on Addressing Root Causes of Migration in Ethiopia.

"Ethiopia is a young country whereby in 2016 the population aged 0 to 29 years stood at 73% and working population (ages 15 to 64) constituted about 53% of the population. However, our (ILO) recent assessment revealed that the current supply of labour is more than the market demand or available employment. There are limited jobs and as a result, youth unemployment is high, and that directly contributes to irregular migration (because of the current migration ban). Lack of decent work opportunities propels the young to migrate abroad in search for greener pastures and better-paying options."

IN NUMBERS

More than three-quarters of the 168,000 returnees from Saudi Arabia (between 2013 and 2014) had irregular status by the time they were deported.

Close to 60% of these returnees migrated irregularly, whereas 15.4% entered Saudi Arabia through legal channels and became irregular due to various reasons, including overstaying their visas.

Source: IOM

According to Ethiopia's MOLSA (the Ministry of Labour and Social Affairs), 480,480 citizens had migrated regularly to the Middle East between 2011 and 2013, prior to the ban. However, many more have migrated irregularly, predominantly victims of traffickers, mainly using brokers from both source and destination countries who facilitate illegal recruitment and labour migration.

18

BATTLING 'EVIL' STEREOTYPES, PREGNANCIES, AND ABUSE IN THE GULF

BY 10 A.M. YOU'VE LOST COUNT OF the number of cups you've had. The Bunna Tetu – coffee ceremony– is sacrosanct. A few polite 'Nos' go a long way in keeping the caffeine overdose in check.

Halewya Said and her mother don't care for the 'no' and thrust a cup of steaming coffee and a slice of soft sponge cake into my hands, displacing pen and notepad.

Halewya has returned to Ethiopia after 10 years in Saudi Arabia. With some business skill training and help with start-up capital, she now runs a bakery that provides cakes to different shops. The money she had saved up in her decade abroad was lost in a bad investment.

In 2005, barely 17, she went to Saudi on an Umrah visa and stayed on undocumented for a decade.

"I was so grateful to come back and see my mother after 10 years. She was very ill. But I was so confused. Dessie had changed so much. I couldn't recognise it," she says of the place she calls home.

"I was excited, too. Everything was different from what I was used to. The air. The utensils in the kitchen, how we cook."

"Ethiopians have a bad name because of a few. Some are considered thieves and killers... I am not like that.

Dessie is 20 km uphill from Kombolcha, and has no mainstream industry to sustain it. Yet, you see long stretches of markets and exchange houses. It's a town pieced together on migrant hopes and money.

"I went with my brother the first time. He stayed there for three years. But I also have sisters who have lived there since 1994 and 2000. They helped me find employers, to move employers, to stay safe, to dodge the police net, as I had no papers."

Halewya is matter-of-fact about her experiences, there's no self-pity, no blame. The first house she worked in she was paid only 600 riyals, but by the time she was with her fifth employer she was earning 1,500 riyals and getting a day off every fortnight.

"I was never scared of my status. Just because I didn't have proper papers I did not hold back while asking for good terms."

She continued to stay in Saudi to pay for her mother's treatment and for the care of her daughter. "Then they announced the amnesty in 2013, and it was time to come back."

So in the mass deportation of December 2013, she came back to Dessie, to make it home, despite how foreign it looked.

"I had saved up 50,000 birrs [less than US$1800] and opened a petty shop. It was a bad decision, without a proper plan. Now with help from some [development] agencies, I have a new business going."

"Because of my religion, people had a positive attitude towards me. Some [employers] are not, they are very bad. I tried telling them, the people there, that even if we are poor, we have families. We don't have modern houses but still have a home. We have fresh food and air. May not be as rich as you, but still have a life," Halewya bites back her tears.

"Ethiopians have a bad name because of a few. Some are considered thieves and killers... I am not like that. My friends and family are not like that. We as a people are good. But how do we make them understand that?"

The negative narrative about Ethiopians disturbs her, and she wonders how that can be changed.

"I am a success. I learnt a lot that I use now. I understand social life. Even if financially I didn't do well, I did do well with my knowledge," she taps her forehead.

Halewya is how Bizuye Fentaw would like her daughter to turn out – with a home, a thriving business, confidence.

It is difficult to believe the tall and youthful Bizuye is the mother of eight children. Momina, who is in the Saudi port city of Jizan, is her seventh child.

Bizuye's home is an altar to the goods Gulf money can buy. Television, stereo system, refrigerator, all covered in the lacy plastic dust covers. The modest facade of the home belies the relative affluence inside. Hers is a rare home that managed to make the best of having family in the Middle East. The kind of home that school girls from impoverished backgrounds, like Imaan, aspire to.

Momina went to Jizan in 2013, when she was just 18. She came home for a holiday last year for four months.

Bizuye's sister has lived there for 20 years with her family and runs a salon, which now employs Momina. She earns 10,000 birrs a month and sends money home every quarter or so.

"I am building a house for her. She got engaged last year to a boy who works in a garage. Once the house is built, and some money put away, then she will come back for good," says Bizuye.

She knows that there's no guarantee Momina's luck will hold.

"It's difficult to talk about her daughter's pregnancy in front of the neighbour. They will gossip."

MOTHER'S GUILT

"My sixth daughter went to Dubai in 2010. She worked for two years, was not paid for one year, and suffered so much abuse. She was paid only 2,000 birr a month when she was paid. Finally, she went to the police and she was sent back empty-handed."

In the room tucked away behind a light curtain are her children and grandchildren. She gazes distractedly in the direction of the muffled banter inside.

"I would not have sent her if she were not working for her aunt," the mother says, offering an unsolicited justification, as she sees us out.

Halewya's mother, who wordlessly refilled the coffee cups, interjected only once, to voice similar misgivings. "My children helped me with my medical treatment. All those stories I kept hearing I was so worried, so guilty. "

Fatima Hassan bears a similar burden – the guilt of the left behind.

Fatima is just 55 and something of an expert on what it means to have your young girls live in a strange country.

She is tired of worrying about her daughters but doesn't see an out anytime in the near future. Of her seven children, two are abroad. Rahma lived in Saudi for 12 years and came back with a son, who is now eight.

"More than two years ago, she went to Dubai." When the ban was in place.

Fatima laughs mockingly. "Ban? The only thing that happens is that the price goes up. Doesn't stop anyone, and the black market becomes profitable. Rahma paid an agent 15,000 birrs to get her to Dubai. "

There's a flurry of activity outside a small window, adjacent to the entryway of her house. A small stool, a large copy machine and a printer are crammed into the space of a closet. A young woman is running the shop. A local government office in the vicinity ensures a steady flow of customers.

The front room of the house, from which the shop has been culled out, has a substantial area set aside for the coffee ceremony Fatima presides over.

ZINA LAW OR 'UNLAWFUL SEXUAL INTERCOURSE'

In the GCC states, 'unlawful sexual intercourse' and pregnancy out of wedlock are punishable offences. This report from Qatar highlights cases of women imprisoned with their babies.

The severity of punishment often depends on the judge. In Saudi Arabia, a domestic worker received an 18-month jail term and was then deported for giving birth outside marriage. In another case, the judge ruled for 90 lashes and eight months in prison.

Single pregnant women who avoid detection by authorities still face complications once they give birth, as the baby will require paperwork, including proof of paternity. Workers like Halewya then resort to sending the baby back home with a married friend or family member.

BABIES ABROAD

"First time she [Rahma] wanted to come back because of the baby. Now the contract is up and she wants to return, but they are not allowing her to."

When Zeba's name is brought up, Fatima looks even more worried, as she has no idea when her daughter will be able to return from Jeddah. Even the amnesty (ongoing at the time of the interview) would not have helped her, Fatima fears.

Zeba was just 16 when she went to Saudi five years ago.

"She ran away and is pregnant. Due any time now... she couldn't seek amnesty.

She is married and lives in her own rented room there. We don't know what will happen to her, or the baby."

It's not easy on Fatima that two of her daughters ended up pregnant while abroad, even though her family is no different from many others in the community.

"Usually the girls send their children with others who are returning and stay back longer to earn more. Then we grandmothers take care of them... they are our babies. But people talk."

Halewya also gave birth to a daughter in Saudi, whom her sister brought back to Dessie to be cared for by the grandmother.

"I was engaged to someone before I went. He also came to Saudi and was without papers. We had a child. After pregnancy, we stayed together."

It's a story you hear often, full of thinly-veiled euphemisms. The fiancé or the husband in Saudi, the child born abroad in secrecy, brought back home to a grandparent... one could read between the lines or accept the story.

Seven years ago Iman, just 16, went to Saudi through a broker. Her mother Ashala last heard from her five months ago. "She came here once, and bought this," she says, unimpressed, pointing to a television that's on when we enter and is likely to remain on through the day. "She never sends money regularly."

"I estimate not less than 30 percent of those who come to Agar are sexually abused."

Their home is one part of a room in a particularly abject part of the slum. A tin sheet separates their family from the one next door. Iman is undocumented and works illegally in Saudi, her father comments, eyes still on the drama on TV.

"She called once five months ago. When she had a baby. We haven't heard from her since," says Ashala, finally beginning to open up. A neighbour walks in and makes herself comfortable, inveigling herself into the private conversation.

Ashala clamps up, her answers becoming more and more non-committal. "No, we haven't tried calling her. She will call when she wants to."

The community worker whispers, "It's difficult to talk about her daughter's pregnancy in front of the neighbour. They will gossip."

Agar Ethiopia, a rehabilitation centre, houses many women who return with a child in tow.

Its Executive Director Abera Adeba says the lack of cultural awareness on both sides leads to harmful stereotypes, like accusing Ethiopian domestic workers of black magic. "And I estimate not less than 30%of those who come to Agar are sexually abused."

The evidence is in the mixed-race children at the centre. It's a reason why many of these women are not accepted back into their communities, and so continue living in limbo at the shelter.

It's not just rape. Many women enter into non-marital relationships that are decried as illegal across the GCC. With no access to reproductive healthcare in these countries and not enough knowledge of their laws pre-departure, the result is that women find themselves in situations that can be criminalised.

TO UMRAH OR NOT TO?

As we walk down the meandering, steep lanes of Dessie, a little girl sitting on the long ledge outside her house waves at us. And just like that, quite unplanned, there's another story to be heard; that of her father's.

Bedru Sofi Abdurahman brings out a small Crayola school bag that holds all his documents, including his daughters' birth certificates and school reports.

He first went to Saudi Arabia in 1988 on an Umrah visa and lived there for 25 years. He found a wife and had two daughters. And was deported three times in that period. Every time, he went back on an Umrah visa, with a new passport. He had the strategy down to a tee.

Then in 2013, when there was the infamous mass deportation of Ethiopians from Saudi Arabia, life became extremely difficult. As the community dwindled, the Ethiopian school there ceased operation.

"My older one who was doing well in school could not continue her education. There was no point living like that there. I could have paid the 12,000 riyals and regularised my status, but I didn't have the money. As a daily labourer, I would earn only 80 to 100 riyals a day."

His wife did not wish to return to Ethiopia, preferring to stay in Saudi irregularly. Now a single parent, and unemployed, Bedru is distraught.

"I have considered going regularly, but that's expensive too... I don't even have savings to send my children to school here."

"I don't recommend people go on Umrah visa," says Halewya. "The cost of living is so high. You pay for everything yourself, which is why I couldn't save much. If you are legal, it's different. The Indonesians on regular visa saved so much in the same period I was there. I could not."

19

FAILED MIGRATIONS AND THE COMMUNITY APPROACH

A YOUNG GIRL, NO MORE THAN 15, CLUTCHES her passport and stands in line at the immigration counter. Her boarding pass says Jeddah. As soon as she clears immigration, an older male and female companion snatch the documents away from her. She doesn't look surprised. Her shoulders stoop under the weight of the airbag that holds all her worldly possessions. The three then join a slightly larger group of women in the waiting area of the departure terminal.

It's a narrative without borders. Migration is a means to an economic end. It is also seen as a protection, to escape domestic violence, poverty and prostitution. It's symptomatic of what happens to girls in patriarchal societies.

Time and time again, across countries, this echoes. Women go abroad to support their families, return with little to their name. This slip of a girl boards a flight, irregularly, to Saudi, even as tens of thousands of others are being deported from the Kingdom for the same reason.

Irregularity not only puts the workers at risk of criminalisation and imprisonment in countries of destination; on their deportation, they also carry with them the stigma of a failed migration.

Daniel Melese, who works on safe migration in Addis and Dessie, says "failed migration is the worst possible outcome. If you've endured hardships and abuse and managed to save and come back on your own terms, then it's still considered a success story."

They go after much struggle, either having gone up against family resistance or by incurring huge debts, so even when they are forcibly returned to Ethiopia, they hide and don't go back to their families, he says.

"You can't even judge the family, as their burden is heavy too."

Many of the psychosocial problems faced by migrant workers are due to unmet expectations, says Aida Awel, Chief Technical Advisor of an ILO project on migrant domestic workers to the GCC.

"They have no idea what they might face, what to do in a challenging situation, and many of them don't even speak Amharic, let alone English or Arabic. Most of them speak other Ethiopian languages, which puts them at a distinct disadvantage."

"They feel they should pretend to be Muslims if they are not, so change their names to reflect a new persona."

Before 2013, pre-departure orientation was a three-hour session at the federal level when they were ready to exit, Awel points out. "Ideally there should be pre-employment training so that one is still in a position to change their mind or take the right decision."

The new Overseas Employment Proclamation, which will lift the ban on citizens migrating for domestic work, emphasises pre-departure training but does not improve the timing and effectiveness of the intervention. The table at the end of this chapter elaborates further on the proclamation's contents.

Agar Ethiopia is a centre which was set up for the elderly 12 years ago, and which now serves as a rehabilitation centre for victims of trafficking who return to Ethiopia.

The large bungalow situated in the more affluent part of Addis can accommodate up to 100 people, but as of late September, had only about 35 returnees including children.

They expect more as the Saudi amnesty comes to an end. "The first phase of amnesty is when those with resources and support return. The mass deportation will happen at the end, and that's what we are preparing for," says Abera Adeba.

Adeba has seen the entire spectrum of abuse that migrants to the Gulf suffer – rape, physical and emotional abuse, and the consequent mental health breakdown.

Agar is home to those who cannot be immediately or easily rehabilitated. A pet dog, a handful of children – toddlers and preschoolers   and their toys provide marginal relief in the otherwise bleak environment.

The staff at the centre are almost all men, with one female nurse on duty. A reminder of the rather strong patriarchal structure of the society.

Many of the residents at the centre are those with extreme mental health issues.

"The causes are not well known. There might be predisposing, perpetuating and aggravating factors. Then there's the provoking factor they face in Gulf states," Adeba says.

He feels the lack of life skills, communication and vocational skills amongst people from rural areas may contribute to this as well.

Not to mention the close-knit community from which they are displaced, to work and live in severe isolation, suffering extreme workload.

"...they [family] think she is a criminal or 'prostitute' or having affairs, and they ostracise them."

Adeba says many of them also undergo a severe identity crisis. "They feel they should pretend to be Muslims if they are not, so change their names to reflect a new persona."

"There is a tendency to migrate among Muslim communities in the region. Probably because of more affiliation. Christians also go. And many change their names and try to pass off as Muslims. Because they feel they will be treated differently. Even wearing the hijab, while getting their passports, even if there is no formal conversion," says Dr Daniel Keftasse of HEFDA.

Though a Christian, Salam had to pretend to be a Muslim. "I don't think they minded, but my relative who found me the job told them I was, so I had to act." Her friend Saba says she had no problems being open about her religion. "They were ok with it, that I was a Christian."

Halewya, on the other hand, felt her religion gave her some protection from the otherwise negative narrative that plagues Ethiopian migrants in the Gulf.

"You learn much from the victims themselves when they come here. Most of the women who come to the shelter live there for three to six months on an average. Some are treated as 'project for life'. The family has invested in them, and when they come back empty-handed, with a child in tow, the taboo doubles and triples," Adeba says.

"When families don't accept them, their mental health takes a further blow. We do counsel the families too. But they think she is a criminal or 'prostitute' or having affairs, and they ostracise them."

Feyise is 25, and her Agar admission papers show she has been there since January of this year. Her recollections are disoriented, and she believes she has been back only for three months. She is from the Oromia region of Ethiopia, the scene of years of conflict.

For the nine months she worked in Beirut, she received no money. She was 'returned to the broker' when she fell very ill, having been denied proper food and overworked.

She could well become the 'project for life' that Adeba mentions.

Aziza Abdul is more lucid in her retelling of the horrible experiences she suffered in Yemen, but her voice is devoid of emotion.

She moved to Yemen 15 years ago and worked as a domestic worker. After five years, she married a Yemeni who physically and mentally abused her. "Then I gave birth to twins. He forced us all to become beggars. I saved money, paid a smuggler and managed to escape. I went to my family, as I wanted to bring my children too. But they left me here [in Agar]."

Aziza doesn't know what became of her children and has lost hope of going back to her family. Every day she is haunted by the memories of what she went through, and of the children she abandoned. She states this as a matter of fact, as if she were speaking of the food she had for breakfast.

There is a pressing need to expand the community conversation because in the coming months, Ethiopia has to deal with thousands of returnees and must prepare for regular migration as well.

In Dessie, mothers come together over the traditional coffee ceremony – The Bunna Tetu – to talk about migration. It's a strategy used during the height of the HIV/AIDS epidemic to teach and engage communities. Now it's being used for safe migration.

Like coffee ceremonies, other traditional groups are co-opted to help with social issues.

The *iddir* for instance. They're informal community insurance groups, and every person or family belongs and donates to their *iddir*. These pre-existing structures, also once used to raise HIV/AIDS awareness, are now speaking about safe migration through pilot projects in select *woredas* in Addis.

The campaigners for these initiatives hope that the message the government is unable to disseminate effectively, due to a lack of trust, will cascade to the community through these groups. That message? To not only accept into their fold those who return in distress, but also to ensure those who migrate don't do so under duress or false promises.

WHAT NEXT AFTER THE OVERSEAS EMPLOYMENT PROCLAMATION?

On 19 February 2016 Ethiopia announced its revised Overseas Employment Proclamation 2016/923 would, when implemented, lift the ban on its citizens migrating for domestic work. The Proclamation on paper is strong. Some of its salient features include:

- *Workers cannot be deployed to a country without a bilateral agreement in place*
- *Workers must receive pre-departure orientation on working environment of the receiving country.*
- *Deployment of these categories of workers is prohibited:*
- *Under 18 years*
- *Without an eighth-grade education certificate*
- *Without a certificate of occupation competence*

There is no mention of the length of training, only that it should be conducted at least three days before departure. The timing is not ideal, as experiences in other sending countries show that the best time to intervene and educate workers is pre-decision to migrate or at least well before recruitment fees change hands.

Asfaw Ambaw, the migration expert from Dessie, sees three main challenges in the migration environment.

"The ban itself is the primary challenge. It was temporary when it was announced, and four years later, though there's a proclamation there's no implementation. People won't wait, so they go in whichever way they can," says Ambaw.

But he's also worried that the country does not have the capacity to handle the implementation of the proclamation, especially the mandatory training, when the ban is completely lifted. "The needs versus the preparation is not encouraging."

And finally, not all the communities in the country have been covered equally.

Though he does not say so, it could well be because of the ongoing conflict in some parts of Ethiopia, where the most vulnerable migrate from.

Afsaw says another problem is that, while the civil society did not play an active role in the drawing of the proclamation, the recruitment agents – an influential group – did.

Once regular migration starts, then the capacity of government structures will have to be built, including a network of labour attaches in missions abroad, he emphasises.

Ethiopia is currently in the process of finalising bilateral agreements with Oman, Saudi, Qatar, Bahrain, Jordan, Lebanon and Kuwait.

The ILO's analysis of the Proclamation highlights the challenges in establishing these BLAs.

One of the factors delaying the conclusion of the agreement pertains to the minimum wages of domestic workers: Ethiopia proposed a minimum wage of 1,200 Riyals, while Saudi Arabia offers 700. Saudi Arabia also requests that Ethiopia ban deported citizens from going back to it. Similarly, the conclusion of a bilateral agreement with the United Arab Emirates is delayed because of the objection to the inclusion of a minimum wage requirement. These difficulties prove the resistance of the recipient countries to according meaningful protection to overseas workers.

"Then I gave birth to twins. He forced us all to become beggars. I saved money, paid a smuggler and managed to escape. I went to my family, as I wanted to bring my children too. But they left me here [in Agar]."

Amy survived on three to four hours of sleep a night for the two-plus years she lived there, with no weekly off.

PHILIPPINES

Published March 2018

POPULATION	100,981,437
NUMBER OF MIGRANTS IN THE GCC	1,335,569
MAIN RECEIVING COUNTRY GLOBAL	Saudi Arabia
MAIN RECEIVING COUNTRY GCC	Saudi Arabia
REMITTANCES (USD MILLIONS)	32,795
REMITTANCES PERCENTAGE OF GDP	9.9%

The Philippines demand for a USD 400 minimum wage for all of its overseas workers led to deployment bans both from the Philippines' and several GCC countries.

20

OUT OF THE PHILIPPINES: IT TAKES A VILLAGE, AND THEN SOME

SHORT OF A KIDNEY, FOR A PRICE, you can buy just about everything outside the POEA complex of offices. Smudge-proof ballpoint pens, waterproof passport covers, low-interest loans, water bottles and snack packs, photography and photocopy services, medical tests.

The service providers are in a long queue that stretches from the gate all the way over the pedestrian overbridge branching out in five different directions. Closer to the gate, the Manila-esque queuing gives way to a dance of vendors, each politely edging the other out to briefly hold the prime spot right outside the gate, where no one can miss what's being hawked.

And between the gate and the main door, a host of other services are available, for free, thanks to a steady flow of aspiring migrants and their families. Some offer, while others seek, help and advice. To fill out forms, to know more about Saudi Arabia, to assure a worried brother that Dubai is not so bad, to exchange Facebook details and to assure a stricken young woman that the Philippines will indeed lift the Kuwait ban and she would be able to fly out soon.

There's an air of camaraderie and in the minutes and hours they spend there, they self-organise into clusters – by the provinces they come from, the countries they are going to, the jobs they are undertaking, the returnees and the newbies.

The advice being shared, especially in the Saudi cluster, is not to go out even if you do get an off day. The off day is already seen as a privilege that only a few may receive. Facebook is the alternative to actual human interaction. Everyone sings paeans to the power of Facebook. The government, the agencies, the workers, the agents. It's surreal, the power being bestowed officially and unofficially on an unsecured social media platform.

The POEA building looks like every government office in Asia, only a little bit more organised, and a lot more obvious in its purpose. The short flight of stairs leads to a lobby and a bank of elevators. Several counters line the wall – banks, insurance companies, financial services. In a small cordoned-off area there's a sales pitch in progress as two spirited youngsters have a group of aspiring migrants enthralled – the magic of remittances.

Becoming an OFW is a community initiative. It truly takes a village. And nowhere is that more obvious than in and around the POEA offices.

Not all of them are waiting to go abroad. There are quite a few who have come to file complaints – on their own behalf or that of a relative.

IN SEARCH OF JUSTICE

Laila has been waiting for a couple of hours. She and her cousin Felix have come to file a complaint and to rescue his sister in Saudi Arabia. This is their fourth visit (between January 15 and February 9) to the offices, and Felix had forgotten the dress code. While he has gone in search of suitable attire to cover up the sleeveless vest, Laila is killing time talking about Nona Fe to whoever is seated around her. She must have recounted the tale a dozen times, still not tiring of it.

Felix comes back, and then more details emerge.

Nona Fe went to work in Abha, Saudi Arabia on 31 December 2017. And from day one her problems started.

"The employer has been pulling her hair and pushing her around. She is overworked and given only one meal a day. They lock her up in the house and lock the refrigerator when they go out," the brother pauses, looking ill at ease.

Laila chips in, "they don't even allow her to use the toilet. They gave her a basin to do her business." There's a whoosh of disapproval from the hangers-on who haven't tired of hearing the story either.

Nona Fe is employed by a large family, with two adjoining homes, where she and another worker take care of everything.

In the initial weeks, she had no contact with her family. She secretly started using Facebook messenger on her Philippines cellphone. Her family pieced together her story over weeks of sporadic messaging. Felix shows the exchange on his phone. There are long gaps in communication. He is bewildered. Why would a human being be treated this way at all?

Felix and Laila first complained to the agency in Manila, who dismissed their concerns saying it was too soon, that she has to adjust and it will get better.

"We have paid for everything. How can we just let it go?" – An agent

ADJUST OR PAY UP

That's the standard advice imparted to workers before they leave and while they are abroad. Nowhere is it reiterated more than at a recruitment agency.

In a side lane, adjacent to the offices of the Commission of Filipinos Overseas, is a narrow three-storeyed building. A signboard announces that this is Hopewell Overseas Recruitment Agency.

A hard-faced security guard demands identification before allowing entry. A few women are shooting the breeze, trying to draw the guard into banter. The ground floor has a few chairs and a gated, locked stairwell inside which there are a few pieces of luggage.

Upstairs is a beehive. Several desks, tiny offices, walls plastered with job notices. Aspiring migrants, mainly women, are sprawled on metal chairs lining the corridors. The wait has been long, it appears.

The agency goes headhunting for household workers in the provinces with permission from the PESO offices. Once recruited, the women are brought to Manila, housed in dormitories run by the agencies, and given the requisite training.

In this office, the Kuwait ban is not yet seen as a dire situation. A recruiter says the problem is in Saudi. "They were dependent on us [(Philippines]) for the service sector. But due to nationalisation, those jobs are dwindling. It was the biggest market for us."

Hazel, higher up in the agency pecking order, interrupts the casual conversation and moves it to the manager's room, now empty of the occupant.

She is suspicious but answers the questions honestly enough.

She says homesickness is the main problem they have to deal with in the case of household workers. "We address it before they go. What's the reason they are going? They should remember that. We also take the family's help to convince the worker to continue working. We don't consider regular complaints as a problem really if it's solved. It's a problem only if they file a formal complaint with the government office."

And despite that, if the worker cancels, the family is asked to pay back the expenses incurred by the recruitment agency. "We have paid for everything. How can we just let it go?"

Exiting the building, the women are still outside, but this time in deep conversation with one another. There's a new member in the group.

"She is supposed to go to Kuwait. We are all ex-abroad, we can go… but she doesn't know what will happen. The agency will not do her paperwork for another country now."

MARKETPLACE FOR DREAMS

Honeywell is just a filament in a tangled network of recruitment. Not too far from here is the Mabini street, in Ermita. It's a marketplace. Glass-fronted offices with a mosaic of leaflets announcing jobs across the world. Many of these doorways are flanked by armed guards. Every job announcement is 'Urgent'. There are more staff outside of the offices than inside. The trick is to lure potential migrants before a neighbouring agency can pin them to a contract. "Immediate visa. Free loan. Want to go to Dubai?" Promises fly around in Tagalog and other dialects.

Non-Filipinos are given a different sales pitch. "Po, how many workers you want? Maid? Sales?" If you are not there to find a job, you must be there to offer some.

It's just a couple of weeks since the Philippines banned its citizens from travelling to Kuwait for work. The environment in recruitment agencies, government office and training centres is fraught. What is to become of those who are one last paperwork away from migrating? There are close to 200,000 Filipinos working in Kuwait, which is a significant market.

Cecille, the interlocutor, is received with curiosity. She is done with agents. She is on the other side now. Helping returning migrants and their families, especially children, to find peace in an uncomfortable reality. Her chosen mode of healing is art. Her journey started 17 years ago when she was just 17. Her father, an OFW who returned from Saudi, sank his tiny savings into drug dealing, and in the bargain, he and his wife became meth addicts. It fell upon Cecille, the oldest, to become the caregiver.

"I went to Japan, to be an 'entertainer'. You know what that means… trafficked, abused, battered... I am healing for and through my children, through my art."

She walks past the agents, recounting her own journey, remarkably without malice or anger.

THE ACRONYM PRIMER

It is a task to remember the names and understand the roles of the various agencies that decide and execute migration policies in the Philippines.

School children and unskilled workers, officials and agents, everyone speaks in seemingly indecipherable sentences dotted with acronyms.

So here's a quick (and nowhere near comprehensive) reckoner of the acronyms used in these stories.

- *CFO: Commission of Filipino Overseas*
- *HSW: Household Services Workers*
- *MHU: Migrant Health Unit*
- *OFW: Overseas Filipino Workers*
- *OWWA: Overseas Workers Welfare Association*
- *PDOS: Pre-departure Orientation Sessions*
- *PEOS: Pre-employment Orientation Sessions*
- *PESO: Public Employment Services Office*
- *POEA: Philippines Overseas Employment Administration*
- *TESDA: Technical Education and Skills Development Authority*

21

TO LEAVE, TO STAY, TO ADJUST… COME WHAT MAY

CLOSE YOUR EYES AND DROP A PIN on a map of the Philippines and voila, you have a community dependent on remittances. These beautiful islands all house hundreds of men and women waiting for a flight out.

The pin drops on Negros Occidental province – in Bacolod, Talisay and Silay – about 700-plus kilometres from Manila.

Sally is something of an icon in this region. Everyone knows her. She is a head taller than everyone around her and has a smile for every emotion – anger, joy, disapproval, irritation.

It is *"ate"* (sister) Sally to the rescue for all things migration. From making sure you are enrolled in a good training centre to ensuring dubious agents don't take you for a ride, from filing complaints about a missing relative to taking an erring agent to task.

It has been 18 years since her return from a 13-year stint in Bahrain, but her experiences are fresh. "Let me tell you, the stories from then are the stories from now," she confides in a mock whisper.

"When I went to the Gulf, Bahrain, Kuwait and Saudi was where everyone went. So I did, too. My first employer was a big businessman. Every morning when I went to make breakfast he would greet me by grabbing my bottom. After two months I called my agency and told them. They called the couple and the wife was shocked.

I was let go immediately."

She didn't want to come back because she had children to put through school and a house to build. So she stayed at the agency and worked for free till they found another employer.

It was then that a wealthy couple looking for a housekeeper hired her. "It was fantastic. They paid me US$110 then, which was a very good salary. She was a diamond trader, my madam. I would travel with her to London and Europe and wear all the jewellery while entering and leaving the countries so that we don't have to pay tax," Sally chuckles at the memory.

She knows her case was not the norm then nor now. "Maybe the amount of abuse has come down. When I was there, 90% of us were treated badly, now 50%."

How does one make a desperate situation bearable? Making the perpetrator(s) pay. [...] the hard truth: they often don't.

She is not willing to give the workers a free pass either. "Sometimes the OFW's personality or attitude is a problem. They go abroad and will do anything for money, to be able to pay off debts... then they get pregnant and come back. At least 25% of Filipinas who go abroad are also forced into prostitution."

These are not figures conjured from thin air. Salvacion 'Sally' Barrios is the President of the Federation of OFW Negros Occidental. Working with potential, current, and returning migrants and their families is her life's work.

She knows every unpaved, unmarked road through the sugarcane fields of Talisay that lead to small, remote settlements. She is privy to the lives of these people, their desires and disappointments, their fears and joys.

"Thirty years ago many went as maids. Still many go. Even professionals, teachers and nurses go and work as maids."

She does acknowledge that there's a shift in behaviour. The children of those who migrated as domestic workers usually don't follow in their parent's' footsteps. It's always from a new group, that's impoverished, not fully literate, arguably choiceless, and hence desperate.

"They sign papers without reading, promising to pay all costs if contract not completed. Or waiving rights to claim damages. They are so eager to leave, they will sign anything. I have a case now where the agency is threatening to file a case against an OFW. I said go ahead. We can fight that."

After dozens of interviews and days of wandering around Metro Manila and the provincial islands of Negros Occidental, there's a pattern that emerges. Resolution and justice first and foremost is measured by the financial recompense. How does one make a desperate situation bearable? Making the perpetrator(s) pay. The agents should pay a penalty. Employers should pay a penalty. Then the hard truth: they often don't.

Baby Ann Fajardo's husband Mark works in Qatar in a once-flourishing catering company – Amwaj – that is now floundering.

It was her brother Louis who first joined the company in 2011 and then found a job for Mark. "I took him there too because in the beginning, it was good. We were paid between QR1,400 and 1,600, given housing and food. Then the management changed and everything went to the dogs," says Louis, who was hospitalised six times due to severe asthma and overworking.

He complained to the POLO in Qatar but failed to recover his dues. "I came back without being paid for the last five months and no end of service benefits. I am owed at least Pesos 70,000 in salaries alone. I've given up hope."

Mark has been in Qatar since 2012. The working conditions have been deteriorating and so has his health. "He is very tired. He works 12 hours without overtime and without an off day. When he falls ill he can't even go to the doctor as there's no medical," says Baby Ann.

Mark is trying to come back, too, but is not sure if he would receive the end-of-service benefits for the six years he put in there.

"There is an illegal trade going on... between employer and illegal agencies in Kuwait." – An agent

THE HEROES AND THE VILLAINS

Honeycel works for a recruitment agency in Kuwait and was holidaying in her hometown of Bacolod when the Kuwait ban was announced. Now that's foremost on her mind. The job contracts on hold, her own job, whether the ban makes sense at all. About 400 domestic worker applications are now on hold for her agency alone.

She is also aware that in the migration ecosystem, her lot is the most maligned. She is not taking that without a rebuttal.

"Many [domestic workers] run away, making alibis, making up stories because they don't want to stay in the house. Six out of 10 times they have no real excuse. They just have friends... some have boyfriends of other nationalities. They are lured to work in salons or at least starts like that, then they end up in prostitution. It is good that Kuwait no longer allows transfer of visa. From visa 20 to 18," she says before shifting track.

"Employers are to be blamed too. We tell them you have three months to return worker if you are not happy. Instead, they return to another agency where they will get more money in return. There is an illegal trade going on... between employer and illegal agencies in Kuwait."

As in Kuwait, so in the Philippines. Patrick Kenneth also feels the problem with 'other agencies'.

He inherited the Bacolod branch of MMML Recruitment agency, one of the biggest in the region. The agency covers all of Negros Occidental province, which includes the main city Bacolod, 12 component cities, and 19 municipalities.

The office is on the first floor of a strip mall in the market area. Recruitment agency banners decorate the railings inside, like festoons.

The timing of the inheritance was not great. With the Kuwait ban, it got even worse, as that was the biggest deploying market for the agency.

"When my father started this business 10 years ago there were fewer than 10 agencies in Bacolod. Now there are 40 to 50. Our space has shrunk."

Patrick feels his business's good practices has in fact worked against them.

There are roughly six to seven steps from interviewing a worker to sending them abroad. The preliminary health test, applying for a passport, sending the bio-data to the agency in Manila, getting the visa and then the one-month training before flying out.

Many agencies send workers to Manila right after the passport is issued. The workers spend months there without income and are made to work informally by the agency.

"We don't do that. We send them to Manila for that last month. We also struggle with retaining workers. We do the initial interview, apply for a passport, and then another agency will give them money and take them away. They don't realise that the money is a trap. Actually a loan. Go, check those posters," he says, pointing to the festoons of advertisements in the verandah.

The posters promise an upfront signing bonus – clarifying, in fine print, that the bonus is really a loan. These 'financial services' provided by agencies clearly defy Philippines' regulations.

Patrick and Honeycel both hint at 'convincing' workers at various points to continue with the migration process or continue working. A change of mind at any point is expensive for everyone involved. It is mandated by the Philippines government that recruitment agents have a Facebook page and are connected to the workers they deploy, pre-departure itself, so the communication between the two parties is easy.

"We ask them (worker and employer) to talk to each other, to settle it. To adjust, if the problem is not too big. I come here to do interviews and conduct seminars with our agency partners. And when they come there I talk to them, too. I remind them why they have come," says Honeycel.

That reminder, as other agencies corroborate, is to take care of the family back home, to realise dreams back home... 'back home' is the stick and the carrot. 'Back home' will suffer if you don't finish your contract. 'Back home' will benefit if you do.

WAR AND NO PEACE

It is Lolly Ann's 25th birthday. She has no particular plans for the day. Just the usual. Cleaning and drying fish, with her partner's mother, to sell in the market later.

She looks wan, and her smile doesn't reach her eyes. The welcome is warm all the same.

Lolly is stoic as she recounts her trauma. Her mother and sister both work in Jeddah. That's where she wanted to go. Lolly was helped by a local recruiter who promised her a job in Saudi. Lolly had no idea where she was headed or how far it would be from where rest of her family was. The vastness of Saudi Arabia was lost on her.

She spent seven months in Manila, being 'trained'. The agency owner found her part-time jobs, so she could be housed in their dormitory and 'trained'.

After seven months there, in October 2016, she got her visa processed, and was set to join her employer in Dammam. But Dammam is not where she would work.

"My employer was good. He took me to Al Awamiyah to take care of his ageing mother-in-law who lived alone there. It was just the old lady and me. Nights the children and grandchildren would drop in. They paid me on time and the promised amount. SR1,500. For nine months I was happy.

They were good to me."

What she didn't know was that their town was the fertile ground for sectarian clashes – between Shia militia and Saudi forces. Lolly still believes that Al Awamiyah is near the Yemen border and that's why it was bombed and that it was the ISIS that conducted door-to- door raids. These are not the facts.

"One day, end of May, there was bombing everywhere. Mamma and I were alone. We were so scared. Then the ISIS came, in uniform, they wanted to take all the men away. Mamma hid me under the bed, so I would be safe. But she was losing her mind. But my employer called and said nothing would happen. They said ISIS just wanted young men and that we were ok. I still panicked."

For four days they lived without electricity. Lolly contacted her family crying for help. The embassy did not know she was in a war zone as her visa was issued for work in Dammam. "The police then came and gave us five hours to gather our things and evacuate the area. We moved to another son's house nearby. I wanted to come back home. I was so scared," her voice rises a few decibels.

Her four-year-old wakes up with a start and reaches out for a cuddle. Lolly holds her close. Leanne was barely two years old when her mother left their home in Talisay.

Leanne was cared for by her paternal grandmother and father during the time her mother was away.

When she insisted on leaving Saudi, her hitherto 'kind' and 'good' employers turned against her. They demanded she pay back nine months salary if she wanted to leave before the end of the contract.

"They complained to POLO and agency, after all those months, that I didn't work properly. They didn't want to give me tickets back home. They didn't pay my last month salary. None of that mattered. I wanted to leave," she says, stroking her daughter's hair.

The bombing continued in Qatif, and Lolly continued to stay there while her paperwork was being processed. She was then moved to the agency in Dammam, where she stayed for one month.

"I had to work in three houses for that favour. The agency owner, the manager of the building where the agency was, and the manager's sibling. I had to work for my food. Not for money."

She came back to the Philippines on 29 August 2017. "I still could not come home straight away. I had no money to come from Manila to Talisay. My family has no money. I waited two weeks there and borrowed money to come home."

Lolly has received one month's salary from the agency in the Philippines as compensation.

"There were so many like me there. Where I lived in Awamiya, the neighbours had Filipina workers too. We were calling for help. Sending Facebook messages... I know I have to leave again, go abroad to work. But I won't go to Saudi. I am scared."

22

RUN SISTER, RUN!

THERE IS A PECULIAR PATTERN IN WHICH experiences are remembered and retold. The need to stitch the story around what went well.

Everyone speaks around the truth. A direct answer requires a lot of probing to pierce the forced congeniality; the temptation to frame abusive practice as cultural differences because what they are told time and time again is 'to adjust' and 'to understand.'

Being privy to a family's deepest secrets places domestic workers in an even more precarious position.

Maricho Aquino, 38, is a mother of four, and can ill-afford to stay in the Philippines without a job. Her husband, like many other men in the bangarays of Talisay, does not have a permanent job. Most men here are daily wage earners, either operating a tricycle taxi or working in the plantations. Her youngest is just two years old and was born after she returned from Qatar in 2015.

Maricho talks about how wonderful her employers were. "I worked in Doha from 2012 to 2015. It was a small family. Three children, the mother and father who worked outside the home. There were two other maids – a Lankan and Indonesian – so work was not too much."

She had signed a contract for USD 400, but did not challenge receiving nearly 40% less than promised. "Madam said come back after contract I will pay you QR2500."

Would she want to?

She shakes her head. "I got pregnant and my boy is so young now. But I want to go back soon. Not to the same employer. I can't. The baba is very angry with me."

Maricho and the other two maids worked without an off day and were not allowed out by themselves, which meant they were witnesses to everything that happened in the house. Every day. Every minute.

"The madam was scared we would run away so she didn't allow us out. Then my contract ended and I wanted to leave. Around that time I saw baba with another woman in the house. I promised him I won't tell madam, but he was still angry with me all the time, and said he would not give me exit permit."

'Madam' came to the rescue, and asked Maricho to 'run away' to the embassy.

"So on 28 April, 2015, I stepped out, but didn't know anything about the city, got scared and came back to the house. But baba saw me on the camera and locked me out. He said I could not come back home. I could not even take my clothes."

Maricho had not received her last salary, did not have her passport, was not given money for tickets and had school fees to pay back home. She found a job with a well-placed Filipino family where she worked for three months (illegally as per Qatar laws), earning double what she did with her official employer.

Once the immediate financial necessities were taken care of, she went to the POLO to seek shelter and after a month came back to the Philippines in September of that year.

A NEVER-ENDING CYCLE

Her oldest, Shaina, is 17 and will soon start college. She is ready for school, smartly turned out in her private school uniform. She was 12 when her mother went abroad, and she helped her grandmother run the house and care for her siblings.

"A lot of my friends were also dealing with the same, so it's not a big deal. I am studying accountancy, there are lots of opportunities for that abroad. So in a few years, I will go too, but for a good job."

Sally says that it's not just casual conversations in school – the curriculum itself discussed opportunities abroad and at home, about training courses, certification. "It's good to have this. To discuss safe migration. They can plan better, assess how relevant what they study is."

She says there just aren't enough employment opportunities in the country. "The country should first invite more investors, to generate more jobs. Then increase the minimum wage. And also with every new government, the policies change." That's as far as criticising the government goes.

It's not just Sally. Most women seem to have a smile for every emotion. The most dreary of stories are told with the upward curve of the lip, a faint dimple, punctuated by a sheepish laugh.

Off the main road, several kilometres inside a wooded area, with scattered lots of sugarcane fields, is a small settlement. The dirt track ends in a flattened piece of land. In one corner, close to the woods, is a basketball hoop. Children and hens run amok.

Amy Bescaser stands outside her sari-sari (petty goods) store, with a hesitant smile, a shy nod. The shop, chicken coop and her home are all encompassed in one misshapen shack with tin sheets and fabric dividing the spaces.

Just over a year ago, she came back from Sharjah after working for 26 months in the emirate.

Her husband is a daily labourer in the sugarcane fields and earns 150 Pesos a day. "That's not enough to take care of my children – 18 and 12 – and the home. My little boy was only seven when I left him with my mother-in-law and husband and went. A neighbour took one month salary as commission and helped me go abroad. My contract said Dhs1500 salary, but I got only Dhs1000."

She worked for a large Iranian family: the matriarch, her four adult children, daughter-in-law, and two grandchildren.

"The children were nice to me, but mama was not. She didn't like giving me any rest. Just more and more work. The children kept pleading with me to stay on as mama was old."

Amy survived on three to four hours of sleep a night for the two-plus years she lived there, with no weekly day off. She considered running away several times but decided against it out of fear of repercussions.

She had to fight to return when her contract ended.

Amy sent all the money she earned back home to build a house. When she came back, little had changed in the community she lives in. "My family is still poor."

A short distance from the shack is an incomplete building. "If I want to finish that, I have to go back."

Maricho and Amy are still seen as the luckier ones. They were paid, even if less than the promised; they 'adjusted' long enough.

Others, like Lolly, have more dire stories.

The shack Grace Bade, 27, lives in with her partner, mother and child is built against the seawall and, come high tide, the house gets flooded, as it had the previous night. The baby is asleep in a hammock raised high enough to avoid the dampness and water rats that might have been washed in. Grace studied computers in Bacolod, but extreme poverty and her father's illness forced her to seek a job abroad.

Jayden was just three months old when Grace left home. After five months at the agency in Manila, she went to Tayma in Saudi Arabia in October 2017.

Her job order mentioned working for a family of five. When she landed there, she realised it was a family of nine – there were seven children ranging from a 16-year-old to a newborn.

"From the beginning, the madam was always finding fault with me. I love her baby, took care of her baby as my own – I had left Jayden behind to go take care of her children so I can give him a good life. She treated me so badly. Angry with me all the time. Nothing I did was enough. She would go through my things all the time, suspecting me. The baba was very nice, but he couldn't help."

Her day began at about 5 a.m. and on a good day ended around 10 p.m., without a break.

"I was not allowed to keep in touch with my family. Did not have a local phone even. They did not give me proper place to stay. There was a storeroom that was really dirty, with a lot of rubbish. I put together three tables and made a bed. The bathroom had no running water."

After three days, Grace told herself that if no rescue was possible, she would have to run away or die.

ON A WING AND A PRAYER

Around the second month of employment, physical abuse began and Grace decided to come back home. "She would keep slapping me on the back. Poking me with her cellphone. Then one day, the 7-year-old came at me with the knife threatening to stab me. I was terrified. Maybe due to the stress, I had started bleeding heavily too, three or four times a month. I had no respite, I was still made to carry heavy stuff up and down the three-storeyed building."

When the workload did not reduce and her request for medical help was ignored, Grace locked herself up in the room, refusing to come down.

"I had two pitchers of water and one kuboos [bread]," Graces chokes up as she recounts the three days of desperation, pain, and hunger.

Meanwhile, Grace's mother, having not heard from her daughter, tried calling her daughter's Philippine's number. By mistake, she 'loaded' talk time to Grace's cell phone instead of her own.

"I had lost all faith. Didn't think I could survive. No food. No water. No contact with the family. When I heard that ping, it was like a message from God. 50 pesos loaded. I texted my mother immediately and asked her to rescue me. She then contacted the agency in Manila."

After three days, Grace told herself that if no rescue was possible, she would have to run away or die.

Late evening on the third day, she heard a knock on the door. "The madam asked me to get my things ready. It was early January this year. I had worked for more than two months but was only paid one month's salary. They were supposed to send SR1000 back home but never gave me a receipt. I had the 500 balance with me. She took that away too. And dropped me off in a bus stop."

A frail and traumatised Grace travelled 17 hours to Riyadh where the agency picked her up from the bus stop. She had to stay there another 18 days, until her paperwork for exit was processed.

Going abroad again is not an immediate option. "If it had not been for my mother... for that bit of luck, I would be dead."

Loreta Egar has valuable advice for her Filipino sisters. "Don't take it lying down. Run away."

"It didn't seem worth it. This t-shirt was more important than what I could feed my family back home for months?"

She has taken the day off from a busy schedule to share her story. She works as a massage therapist, runs a frozen food business from her home, and is an Avon sales lady. Those are her day jobs, when she is not caring for her children and mother.

"I am not going back abroad," she declares as she sits down for lunch, pulling out from her handbag a toddler's t-shirt and shorts with the Ferrari logo emblazoned on it. "This is a reminder for me."

She went to Dubai in April 2017, through friends of friends who have an agency – 'backdoor' as she puts it.

"I thought it was easier to go this way. You have to pay more money if you went regularly. And also spend months in Manila on training. A relative in Dubai whom I trusted helped me."

She landed in Dubai on a tourist visa and stayed at the agency there for three days. On the fourth day, she met her first employer, who paid the agency Dhs 15000 (USD 4000+) and took her home. "He said he will observe me and then process my visa. I was promised Dhs 1200. There were two Sri Lankan maids too. They had three children. They were horrible. The parents would hit them to discipline them, but nothing worked. I couldn't stand it. They kept shouting the whole day. Fighting with each other. Then one day the young boy hit me."

Loreta insisted on being taken back to the agency, where the 'madam' and agency employees tried convincing her to go back and work. "Madam kept saying it was an accident and that I was lying. They didn't want to listen to me. The agency was very angry with me and shouted at me. Because now they have to give back the money to the family."

She waited for another employer and during that time decided if she had a problem again, she wouldn't come back to the agency because of their abuse.

The second family she was employed with were a couple and their two-year-old. "They didn't have room in their apartment so I had to stay in the house of their mother and sister, sharing a room with their Indonesian maid. My madam would bring the baby over during the day and I would take care of him. They were very nice to me. The mother and sister were not."

They would shout and swear at the Indonesian and Loreta. Loreta was whacked with pillows. The Indonesian was slapped on the back. It was daily abuse. They worked without an off day from 5 a.m. till past midnight.

"Then one day while pressing clothes, I ran the iron over this," she says, clutching the t-shirt, pointing to the print on it.

"For this they deducted Dhs 1000 from my salary of Dhs 1200, and threw the baby's clothes on my face. That was it. It didn't seem worth it. This t-shirt was more important than what I could feed my family back home for months?"

The day after, on 2 October, she left the house with her handbag and the clothes she had brought with her from the Philippines, leaving behind the gifts she had received and her passport, which was with the employer.

"I took this t-shirt and shorts as a reminder. I decided to go to the labour office, but I didn't know the city. I was running away... I flagged down the first car that came my way and asked the two men inside to help me. To take me to the embassy."

That's when, according to Loreta, her 'guardian angel' appeared.

A big, white car stopped the car she was in and a man wearing a kandura got down. He instructed the two men to let her out, asked her to get into his vehicle, and gave her a patient hearing. When he asked her where her employer's home was, Loreta says her heart was racing so fast she thought she would collapse. She was terrified he would take her back.

"Then he turned in the opposite direction and drove away. He saved me. He went through my bag to make sure I had not stolen anything. I don't know why I trusted him. He said if I had my passport he would have paid for my ticket and taken me directly to the airport, but now he had to take me to the embassy."

Loreta assumes he could have been the police or CID or an official. "He warned me that the two men could have taken me to the desert, forced me into prostitution, taken me as a sex slave, left me for dead... these things happened so often, according to him. I was lucky to escape. I sent up prayers, for sending this man here when I needed help."

In the six months Loreta worked there, she saved nothing because she had to keep sending money home for her mother's medicines, her brother, and her children's upkeep. "I am a single mother. I am just grateful I came back alive."

She worries for the Indonesian working in that household. "She was already in a bad shape. And she was not strong. She really had no choice. A big family, all dependent on her."

She also wishes her Filipino sisters have what she had... the strength and resolve to escape. "Run away to the embassy. Nothing is worth enduring abuse."

23

MARKETING THE 'WORLD CLASS FILIPINO WORKER'

THE PHILIPPINES STATE MACHINERY IS WELL-OILED, REGULARLY tuned and intimately aware of the terms of engagement in the global labour market. It anticipates needs from Asia-Pacific to West Asia, from Europe to Africa. Those needs are then deftly met and quickly delivered to a global migration platform that is so pockmarked that any semblance of order or organisation becomes a benchmark.

Order. That's a thought that will catch you unawares in the chaos of Metro Manila. For a sprawling city so densely populated and not really wealthy (the massive billboards and huge malls at every turn notwithstanding) there is an inexplicable order – fairly clean, fairly structured, fairly respectful of each other – and it becomes fairly clear why its citizens are sought after in many parts of the world to run the services and retail sector, to take care of the young and the elderly.

"World Class Filipino Worker." That's the official tagline for the Philippines' marketing spiel. A blatant commodification of its citizens.

It's a spiel that works. Learning to serve. A session at the training centre

The Technical Education and Skills Development Authority (TESDA) holds a place of pride in this marketing campaign. It's a straight sell: "We expect better wages because we will provide well-trained workers."

Celestino Millar is a specialist with TESDA's planning office. He says it's a continuous dialogue with both the industry and the POLO recommendations to provide relevant training that gives Filipinos an edge in the international labour market.

There are no GCC-specific certifications provided, though there is an agreement with Saudi, partnering with the Kingdom's Technical Vocational Corporation, to ensure the standards are in accordance with their needs in construction, electronics and metal work, says Celestino.

There are about 4,000 authorised training centres spread across the archipelago of over 7,500 islands. Of these, 91% are privately run. Audits are conducted, and licences revoked, according to officials. It is a mammoth task making sure the most remote training centres still meet standards.

It's probably why they have made it mandatory that the most vulnerable of the lot, the 'household service workers,' train at the main centre.

The Philippines understands that better skills training would mean better wages – and the elephant in the room, higher remittances. It is now working on TESDA-certified training in countries of destination, so workers' aspirations don't have to end with landing their first job abroad.

"We want them to go from being domestic workers to caregivers; to cosmetologists; to aspire to develop and improve their career choices," an official says.

Master Global is a TESDA-certified training centre in Bacolod, in a large brick and glass structure, still smelling of fresh paint and varnish. They provide training in sheet metal work, spa and cosmetology, cooking and Food & Beverage services.

REMITTANCE ECONOMY

As of August 2015, the national population stood at 100.98 million, with 9.1 million in the diaspora. According to statistics from 2015, over 5,000 Filipinos leave the country every day. Saudi, UAE and Qatar figure in the top 10 destination countries.

It is the third largest remittance receiving country in the world after India and China and ahead of Mexico, receiving $31.14 billion in 2016. That is over 10% of its GDP.

These certificate courses are not designed just for labour export, but also to fill national vacancies. There are scholarships given by local governments and there are drop-in admissions as well.

An F&B class is underway, with about 30 students. More than half have family in a Gulf state and all but one are determined to go abroad to work. Finding local employment, even though there is a local tourism sector that seeks qualified candidates, is not an option for these students.

In an adjacent room, about a dozen youngsters are being trained to take an order and serve in a restaurant. The emphasis is on bending low, smiling a lot – mistaking saccharine sweetness for good service.

Is that part of the export package? Service with a smile, whatever the cost?

Before the TESDA certification, there's also the Pre-Employment and Pre-Departure Orientation sessions (PEOS/PDOS) for certain category of workers.

Migrants comply with PEOS/PDOS with very little understanding or appreciation of why they need this. These trainings do not speak of rights. All the adjustments [are] expected from the worker."

REQUISITES DON'T EMPOWER

Maria Regina, officer-in-charge on the Commission on Filipino Overseas, insists it is not the state's policy to send people abroad for economic reasons, that the government merely respects the right to move.

"But that's not what people understand. There are unfulfilled national vacancies in healthcare, BPO sectors, for teachers and nurses… Yet, doctors get nursing certificates to go abroad. Teachers go as domestic workers. We are trying to lure teachers back to the country, those who work as household workers in the Gulf and Asia-Pacific."

Ellene Sana of Centre for Migrants Advocacy is not completely sold on the orientation sessions or the skilling certifications. According to her, the training and certification are all to justify the USD 400 minimum wage, and not in any meaningful way to empower workers.

"Migrants comply with PEOS/PDOS with very little understanding or appreciation of why they need this. These trainings do not speak of rights. They only say 'be obedient', 'don't annoy your employer', 'try to accommodate', 'don't complain too much'. All the adjustments [are] expected from the worker," she says.

Johnny Plaga worked in Saudi for nine years and is proud of the very reputation Ellene finds problematic.

Though not a fan of the Middle East, he says Filipinos are in great demand. "We are good, hardworking, disciplined, obedient, and avoid 'gir-gir' (gossip). We get our salary and send money home."

Ephifanio Enojo, a recent and proud homeowner, has spent many years abroad. The most recent stint was in Saudi for a couple of years. He echoes a similar thought. "There is some harassment. But you follow their rules there's no problem. Just follow."

Hardworking. Discipline. Obedience. Remittance. The total package, stripped of the softer nuances of what it means to live and work in a strange country that will never be home.

PRICE OF LONELINESS

Johnny's is considered a successful migration. He went, he earned, he saved, wasn't duped and returned. Doesn't stop him from tearing up when he talks of the years he spent away from his family.

A pipe-fitter, he developed debilitating back pain within a few years of landing in Saudi. "Some days I would have to crawl, because I could not stand up straight. But I had to work, my daughter had to finish her education."

Overwhelmed, he excuses himself for a bit. His wife says, "we could hear the pain in his voice when he called us, but we could only cry. Even now, he suffers."

Once their daughter completed her education and started working – in a real estate firm in Bacolod city – Johnny returned. Does his daughter have her sights set on the Gulf too?

The hitherto soft-spoken Plaga becomes agitated. "I don't like the Middle East. I will not send my daughter there. The Filipinas there... they take temporary marriage contracts. And the men I worked with some lost touch with their family. It's not a place to live alone like that."

Abigail Compusto knows the price paid for that kind of loneliness.

She lives a couple of hours out of Metro Manila with her daughter. Her husband Romelle has been in Dammam, Saudi since 2011. She is stuck between a rock and a hard place. "I know he is very lonely there, that's why he is with another woman. I want him to come back here so we can start over. Lately, he has been finding it very difficult. He wants his family."

Romelle works 13 hours a day in two establishments run by his employer – a cleaner in a hospital in the morning and a 'tea boy' at a regular office in the evening.

"It's at the hospital that he met her. He knows it's dangerous there to have affairs, but he is so alone. I am trying to forgive and give one last chance. The last time I gave a chance it didn't work. He came to Philippines with her... she is from

Mindanao. I am still hurt."

Abigail is not fully dependent on him. He sends 15,000 pesos a month which she saves for their daughter. She runs her home with the income she earns as a beautician. "If he comes back without her, we will start a food processing business, catering, start afresh."

Divorce is not legal in the Philippines and annulment is an expensive and complicated process. So couples persist despite extramarital affairs and personal turmoil.

Many of the people interviewed chose to live together as a family unit without a sanctioned marriage. In an otherwise complex web of patriarchal systems, religious proscriptions and economic compulsions, creating family units outside the gridlines is simple and accepted.

Especially in the case of OFWs – it's almost expected that either the one who leaves or the one left behind, or both, are likely to enter into alternative relationships of convenience.

ACKNOWLEDGEMENTS

THIS SERIES WAS POSSIBLE THANKS TO THE GENEROUS CONTRIBUTIONS OF:

Hivos International
Swiss Agency for Development and Cooperation
Pro Victimis
Open Society Foundations

AND MANY THANKS TO THOSE WHO WERE GENEROUS BOTH WITH THEIR INSIGHTS AND THEIR NETWORKS:

Association for Stimulating Knowhow, India
Bandana Pattanaik, GAATW
Benil Thavarasa, SDC, Sri Lanka
David Des Dicang
Ellene Sana, CMA, Philippines
Father Churchill, South Asian Fishermen Federation
Grameen Development Services, India
ILO in Africa
Kanak Dixit, Himalay
Laxman Basnet, SARTUC
Marie Apostol, Fair Hiring Initiative, Philippines
Migrantcare, Indonesia
Somprasad Lamichhane, Pravasi Nepali Coordination Committee
Sr Josephine Valarmathi, National Domestic Workers Movement
Yasin Kakande

BIO

Vani Saraswathi is the Associate Editor and Director of Projects at Migrant-Rights.org.

She moved to Qatar in 1999, where she worked with several local and regional publications and launched some of Qatar's leading periodicals during a 17-year stint. She also reported regularly on human rights issues in Qatar for publications in India. During her stay in Qatar, she and some likeminded people mobilised a grassroots community to help migrants in distress.

After nearly 20 years as a journalist in mainstream media, she joined Migrant-Rights.org in 2014. At the grassroots level, she organises advocacy projects targeting individual employers, embassies, recruitment agents and businesses in Qatar, Kuwait, Saudi Arabia and UAE, working with nationals and long-term residents in these countries.

She reports for MR and is responsible for the Stories of Origin series, which explores the lived experiences of migrants and families in home countries. The idea is to personalise these stories and people for the Gulf audience and to help change the negative narrative surrounding migration in the GCC states.